AF243707

Web Project Survival Guide

Real world tips for bringing projects in on time, on budget

Stan Shinn

RareClarity, LLC
Dallas, TX

Web Project Survival Guide

Real world tips for bringing projects in on time, on budget

Published by:
RareClarity, LLC
120 East FM 544
Suite 72 PMB 354
Murphy, TX 75094

Phone: 866-727-3252
Fax: 888-432-5796
orders@stanshinn.com
http://www.stanshinn.com

All rights reserved. No part of this book may be reproduced or transmitted in any form or any means, electronic or mechanical, including photocopying, recording or by any information storage and retrieval system, without written permissions from the author, except for the inclusion of brief quotations in a review.

This publication is designed to provide accurate and authoritative information in regard to the subject matter covered. It is sold with the understanding that the publisher is not engaged in rendering legal, accounting, or other professional services. If legal advice or other expert assistance is required, the services of a competent professional person should be sought.

The author and RareClarity shall have neither liability nor responsibility to any person or entity with respect to any loss or damage caused, or alleged to have been caused, directly or indirectly, by the information contained in this book. If you do not wish to be bound by the above, you may return this book to the publisher for a full refund.

Unattributed quotations are by Stan Shinn.

Copyright © 2004 by Stan Shinn. All rights reserved.

Printed in the United States of America.

Publisher's Cataloging-in-Publication
(Provided by Quality Books, Inc.)

Shinn, Stan.
   Web project survival guide : real world tips for bringing projects in on time, on budget / Stan Shinn.
   p. cm.
   Includes index.
   ISBN 0-9740652-1-8 paperback
   ISBN 0-9740652-2-6 e-book
   1. Web site development. 2. Project management. I. Title.

TK5105.888.S487   2004
005.2'76   QBI03-200717

About the Author

Stan Shinn has extensive business development and IT leadership expertise in managing fast-paced, growth-oriented organizations. His rare blend of entrepreneurial business acumen and IT expertise foster innovative approaches to technology, resulting in business growth and market success.

He has a proven record of success in Fortune 500, midsize, and hyper-growth, pre-IPO companies. His experience includes technology leadership positions at TechSkills, Edgia, NetCertification, OnNet, Context Integration, and MetaSolv Software.

Stan's technology leadership capabilities include technology roadmapping, systems integration, highly complex backend integration projects, database and security infrastructures design, and implementing high-end, high-availability, fault-tolerant e-Commerce systems built on open technologies. He has significant expertise managing multi-divisional client projects.

Stan's creativity, talent and passion for Internet marketing inspire him to excel in the areas of permission based marketing and online product sales systems. Customer response rates from these campaigns routinely beat industry averages.

Stan obtained his BS in Computer Science at the University of Mary Hardin-Baylor, and his MTS from Phillips University.

Table of Contents

Introduction

In order to implement projects successfully, we must use project methodologies that give us standardized templates for crafting and managing projects in a cookie-cutter fashion. Repeating the success of past projects requires us to formulate a method to duplicate these past successes.

> **In today's tough business climate, you cannot afford costly project failures.**

Web consultancies have crafted methods to manage web projects in a repeatable way to reduce risk and maximize success. Most web-consulting firms keep such techniques internal; it is proprietary intellectual property they leverage to gain competitive advantage. This book reveals those secrets.

■ SECRETS OF SUCCESS REVEALED

Most software development methodologies were created to manage projects lasting three to nine month; many are optimized for even longer projects. Web projects are typically delivered in less than ninety days.

In today's competitive business climate, you cannot afford costly project failures. This book provides real-world advice to bring projects in on time, on budget. Propel your career by mastering the keys to project success! Learn how to:

- Create adaptable project plans.
- Build web systems that scale.
- Choose the best vendors.
- Negotiate the most favorable agreements.
- Produce web designs end users like and use.
- Solve problems as quickly as they occur.
- Accurately estimate project timelines and costs.
- Avoid common mistakes and wasteful expenses.
- Outwit competitors to achieve market dominance.

Take command of the factors spelling success—right from the start!

Stan Shinn

1 Optimism Meets Reality

"I don't get it," the project manager complained. We were debriefing after a project launch debacle, and tensions were running high. "We had our best people on the project. We authorized overtime. We even had outside consultants review our systems before we put the system into production. And now this!"

My boss was referring to the high-profile new system we had spent months building—only to have our customers utterly reject it. We had worked hard, planned extensively, and spent hundreds of thousands of dollars to develop what was supposed to be a revolutionary system to save millions of dollars for the company.

Yet we had failed.

Even worse, there were no assurances we would fare any better on the next project.

Does this scenario sound familiar? Multiple studies indicate the failure rate for custom software projects is above 60%. This astonishing statistic is tolerated only because software systems are integrally vital to modern organizations. Given this poor track record it is no wonder businesses balk at increasing IT budgets.

Why do these failures occur? Software projects fail not from lack of effort, but from effort misguided. A nimble, easy-to-use methodology makes projects consistently successful.

■ TECHNICAL SUCCESSES; BUSINESS FAILURES

Consider a less-than-successful project in which you've participated. Did the project run aground because the developers didn't know how to program?

Projects can be technical successes but business disasters. Ask any end user who patently rejects the software IT has labored to produce for them, and they'll quickly say —"This software isn't what we needed!"

Thus the problem. Typically, at project kick off end users are asked what they need. Then IT goes off for a few months, and after the rigors of quality assurance testing, the end users finally get their hands on the software.

Now, the user gives *real* feedback, but it's too late. You've already exhausted the budget and timeline for the project. More time and funding are needed to add the features end users really need, but it is too late to recover. The abacus ticks off another failed IT project. The only thing saving you from losing favor is IT's pre-existing perception as a fickle monster, fed often but only intermittently able to deliver high-impact, successful systems.

■ ADAPT OR DIE

Want to break out of this vicious cycle? Fortunately, the rise of Internet technology has forced IT to adopt new methods that inherently combat the issues leading to failed projects. Delivering web systems rapidly to a geographically dispersed customer base is requiring dramatic changes to the way software is constructed and managed.

Today's new economic structure is characterized by compressed business cycles. Companies are increasingly under pressure to launch new products or services in mere months from conceptualization. In the war of business, bringing new IT solutions to bear on the market is not just a perk—it is a business necessity.

Businesses must adapt new ways of managing projects—or go out of business. The 60% failure rate is simply no longer a viable option.

■ FRIENDS DON'T LET FRIENDS MISMANAGE PROJECTS

Project plans lay out a defined series of steps to accomplish a goal. Most software development methodologies produce an undesirable goal—failure. The 60% failure rate is not just dumb luck, it is the natural consequence of the methodology. To change the outcome, we must change our methodology!

I've witnessed failed projects which did not achieve business results. Despite experience and planning, many times the best efforts still turned into the worst results. Developers typically lack a good road map to navigate their project to a successful end. This lack of direction dooms the project before the first line of code is even written.

Don't become another victim of project failure—adopt a proven software development methodology!

Chapter 1 Summary

Technical Successes; Business Failures

- The failure rate for software projects is above 60%.
- Projects can be technical successes but business disasters.

Adapt or Die

- New web methodologies inherently combat the issues leading to failed projects.

Friends Don't Let Friends Mismanage Projects

- Developers typically lack a good road map to navigate their project journey to a successful end.
- Lack of direction dooms a project before the first line of code is even written.

2

Delivering Projects at Web Speed

Business changes quickly. Today's business cycles are compressed—companies demand solutions requiring delivery in record time.

In order to meet changing business needs, project management must be be flexible, adaptable, and above all quick! Break web projects into a series of iterations delivered in less than three month cycles. This enables you (at reduced cost and risk!) to deliver business solutions that address quickly evolving business needs.

■ THE NEED FOR SPEED

Project management must balance the triangle of cost, quality and time. With web systems, project managers find themselves scrambling to deliver innovative solutions while still controlling costs.

The rapid pace of change and innovation on the web has caused a new catch phrase to be coined—'Internet-time.'

Doing things in Internet-time means getting things done faster than in the old economy. The rapid rate of e-business change makes quickly delivering web solutions imperative.

Who Needs this Methodology?

Anyone building a business web site benefits from using this methodology: decision makers, business managers, web project managers, technical team leaders, consultants, digital media directors, and most of all, the web developers who are often left to improvise and manage projects with little direction from their management.

Legacy Methodologies

In the late 1980s the advent of Client/Server technology as a new technology platform caused new methods of software delivery to be created. Host-based systems relied on mainframe technologies and centralized systems centered around 'waterfall' methodologies. Project implementation often took nine to eighteen months or more.

Client/Server Methodologies

Client/Server technologies focused on creating decentralized PC-centric systems. Client/Server systems emerged to facilitate building RAD (rapid application development) methodologies. Most of these development methods focused on an iterative, staged-delivery approach.

The Client/Server project was broken into multiple phases each containing a complete iteration. Prototyping, coding, quality assurance, and end user evaluation took place within each iteration. Since software was being rolled out in phases, each stage could be evaluated and major system flaws detected early in the life cycle.

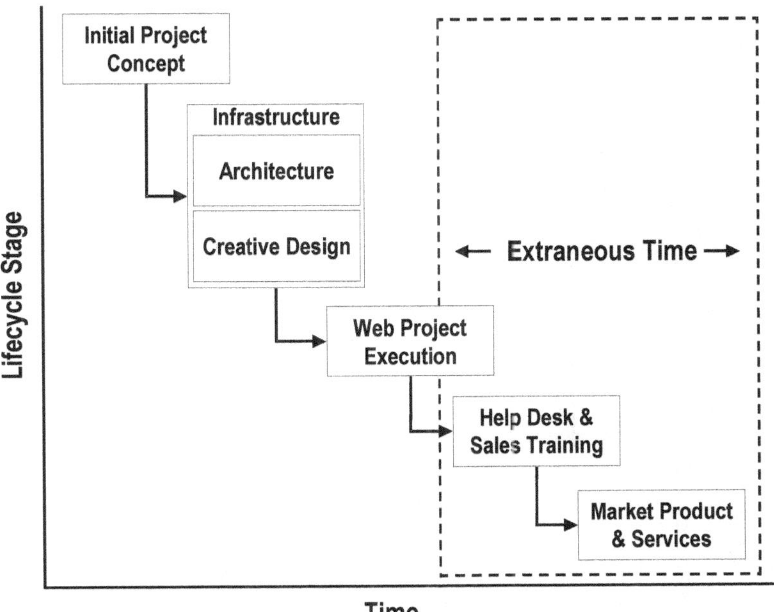

Client/Server Iterative Methodology

Web Era Methodologies

Web systems are deployed not in the nine to eighteen month cycles of the Mainframe era, nor in the three to nine month cycles of the Client/Server era, but now take place in a mere 30 to 90 days!

Many of the characteristics of both the Waterfall method and the Iterative methods are not possible in sub-90 day projects. The days when gathering requirements took three months are now replaced with an economy that demands web solutions be delivered—from start to finish—in only three months!

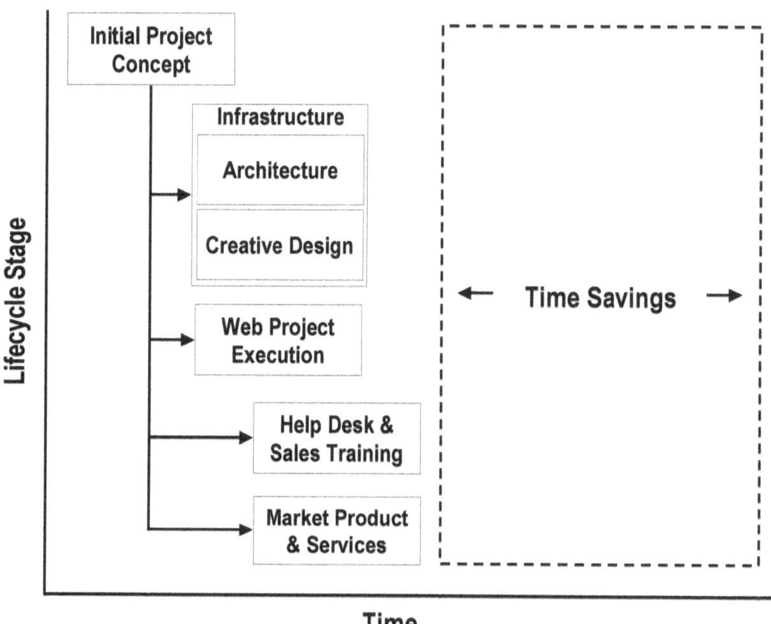

Web Speed Methodology

The new web economy has provided web developers with tools allowing them to react more quickly and accurately to new requirements and a changing business environment. Gone are the days when you have to schedule to install software on an end user's PC and take a week or two to get feedback. Web developers quickly whip together a web page, review it with an end user, and start to work on its back-end code all within the span of a few hours, thanks to web browsers and Internet collaboration.

Just as web developers have quickly adapted to the new economy, web project leaders have found new project management techniques are needed to facilitate delivering web projects on time and on budget in short 30 to 90 day life cycles.

■ ADVANTAGES OF WEB SPEED

The main drive to deliver web systems in 30 to 90 days is competition. With rival companies delivering services in Internet time, businesses must beat the competition to market with new products and services.

Reduced 'Ceremony'

Shorter life cycles have less overhead. Project life cycles lasting six to nine months or more require a larger degree of administration and project management to ensure projects are faring as expected. To ensure the projects are on time, on budget, and meeting objectives, traditional project management methods employ large degrees of 'ceremony'—having lots of meeting, documents, administrative controls, and sometimes painstakingly tedious process detail.

The percentage of time spent on administrative overhead in longer life cycle projects is considerably more than in 30 to 90 day projects. A project spanning nine months might require 20% administrative overhead. Web projects done in less than 90 days require often only 5 to 10% administrative overhead. Low ceremony equals lower costs.

Element	Traditional Project	Web Project
Schedules	Fixed delivery dates; longer project cycles	Flexible delivery dates; aggressively short project cycles
Style	Linear and rigid release schedule	Parallel and iterative development
Project Management Skills	Focused on controlling schedule and cost; less involved in implementation and technology	Broad range of technology skills as well as soft skills; less emphasis on procedure and ceremony
Change	Formally controlled; rigid project plan rejects most change requests	Market driven; changes happen at all stages of life cycle and are accepted
Tools and Technology	Risk adverse; tends to follow proven technologies	Innovative and 'bleeding edge' technology adoption
Definition of Success	Brought in on time and on cost	Addressing market demand in a rapid fashion; innovation and time to market are more important than meeting rigid delivery dates

Traditional Projects vs. Web Projects

Agility to Adapt

Technology evolves quickly. Within six or nine months of a project delivery, the market may produce entirely new platforms radically altering your build-vs.-buy decisions. Delivering solutions in 30 to 90 day cycles enables regular reassessment of business assumptions.

Projects spanning nine months or more tend to be inflexible. Most project managers are not interested in reworking the base assumptions of an elaborately crafted massive project plan. By contrast, web solutions that are delivered in 30 to 90 day life cycles allow a business to quickly change course and take advantage of newly released technology solutions. Remain competitive by delivering with web speed in an ever-changing market.

Only Essential Features are Built

Not only do end users often not know what they want, they often think they need features that are really non-essential. Systems delivered in short time frames provide quick feedback from real-life end users' experiences with the software.

Cost Effective Staffing Model

The shorter cycle of the web delivery model allows the use of a relatively flat staffing model for most of the project. Traditional projects often have a bell-curve shaped hiring plan. Initially, the project consists of mainly business analysts. It later grows to add technical architects and database designers as the project moves into detailed design. Nearing construction, the project finally adds a team of developers. This bell-curve hiring model means constant training to educate new team members.

The web staffing model envisions the entire project team on board typically within two weeks of project inception. Since prototypes and other development begin almost immediately and concurrent with much of the backend design, the staffing model remains fairly flat. This smooths out cash flow, simplifies hiring, training, and reduces the overall cost to develop systems relative to traditional methods.

■ THE COST OF UNNEEDED FEATURES

Studies have shown the cost to initially build a piece of software is only a fraction of the total lifetime cost of the software. Each feature implemented must be supported and maintained for months or even years. Each time you change platforms, upgrade systems, or adopt a new application server, the feature must be tested and possibly modified to work in the new environment.

A whopping 50% to 80% of the lifetime cost of a feature is spent in this maintenance mode.

So what does this mean? Unneeded features are not cheap—they are dangerously expensive! That feature the users 'probably want' only took three weeks to build, but a week to test and deploy, and (over the next four years) an additional 16 weeks to maintain and support. That's 20 weeks of real cost. That feature that took 3 to 4 weeks to build costs nearly half a developers annual salary once you've amortized the support costs!

To control software costs, eliminate unneeded features costing two to five times more than the initial development expense. Use a ruthlessly draconian approach to building only what is absolutely needed, building it in short cycles, and seeing what end users really want and need before expending precious corporate resources.

■ BUILT TO ORDER SOFTWARE

End users ask for features based on what they *think* they need, but in reality, only about 20% of what people are asking for are things they absolutely *have* to have to get the job done. The other 80% of the features might be nice to have, but are non-essential. Roll out a small set of features in the initial release. The rest of the features are cataloged and delivered "just-in-time."

The just-in-time phrase was coined originally in manufacturing. Components were delivered just-in-time from the suppliers only once the customers requested a product. Computers, for example, could be configured within a matter of days or hours as the computer manufacturer requested the parts from various suppliers and quickly assembled the product on-the-fly.

For the manufacturing industry, it was revolutionary to streamline the delivery process by delivering components just-in-time. We now hear about this concept applied to other markets such as the software industry, with it's just-in-time compilers that compile software code on the fly at run time as you need it.

The just-in-time notion can also be applied to the way projects are structured. By compressing project timelines into 30 to 90 day cycles, your business becomes nimble enough to adapt to changing market conditions.

Just-in-time software delivery says in essence: "We'll deliver features once the customer has demonstrated this is truly a requirement, not just a nice-to-have feature."

Judging market conditions nine or twelve months out is tricky. With longer project life cycles you commit to building a comprehensive set of features that will not be available for several months. By the time the system is delivered, the market will have changed, often radically.

Delivering systems in sub-90 days chunks allows you to react and 'fine-tune' the product roadmap.

Consider the astronauts of the Apollo missions. Physicists calculated months in advance the trajectory and landing site for the Apollo astronauts to land on the moon. But as the astronauts made their heart-pounding landing, they engaged in numerous last-minute course corrections, firing thrusters in short bursts in their descent. No amount of research gives perfect information. Fine tuning your plan on an ad hoc basis as conditions change produces success.

Likewise, no one knows with certainty what market conditions will be present in nine or twelve months. Shorter project cycles mean more flexibility to adapt and succeed in a competitive market place.

■ MANAGING SOFTWARE ON DEMAND

So how do you develop and manage just-in-time features? Keep a well-defined list of the requirements requested from end users. Catalogue each of these requirements with a level-of-effort assigned to each item.

When you have collected your list of requirements you essentially have a "menu." This is a list of software features you can add later, à la carte.

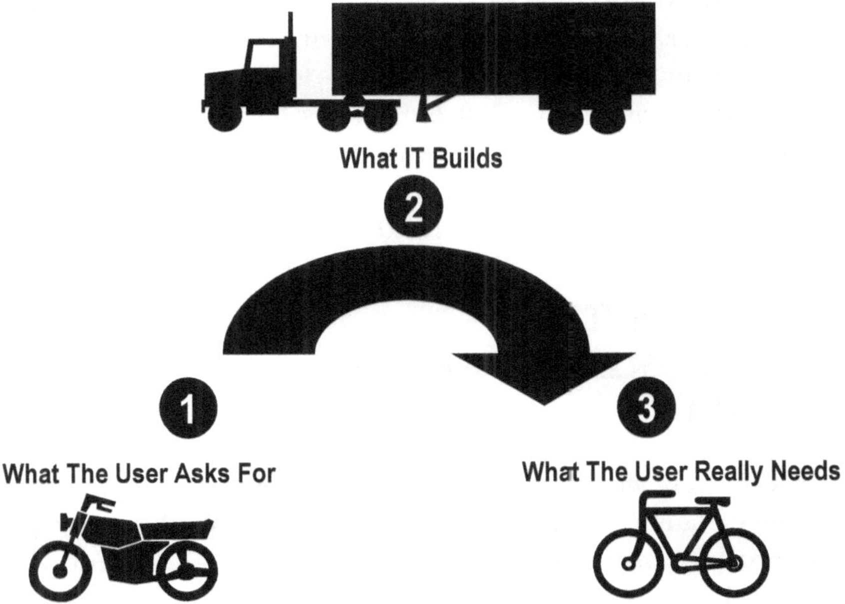

Just-in-time Approach

For example, let us say you are building a commercial software package. You supply this list of features to your sales staff and you'd say: "We could deliver these particular software features in one month. These next set of features take two weeks apiece to deliver. The last four features are mammoth, four month items requiring further research." Because there is a level of effort assigned to that particular feature, you associate a cost to each item. People think to themselves, "Okay, if I could sell this particular service to someone, and they really need this feature, I could add this feature into the price of the proposal I'm giving to this person. Of course, we have to check with IT to see what the actual calendar delivery date is, but I can see it's about a month's worth of work—I could probably have this feature in two or three months if I sell it."

By giving them a list of build-to-order features, developers empower salespeople to have an inventory of software features they can sell—just-in-time—to customers.

A just-in-time feature list empowers end users. IT begins to say, "All of these things are things we *could* do, but what we need to do is see these features be a demonstrable business requirement before we fund their development."

■ JUST-IN-TIME FEATURES EVERY 90 DAYS

In this new world, salespeople lose one more excuse not to deliver sales. They won't be able to say, "Well, I can't sell this product because it doesn't have features X, Y, and Z." Rather they're given a list and told, "When you sell this product, we'll deliver features X, Y, and Z within three months." Simply bump up the price of the product or service to include the development of these extra items, and you're on your way to new sales, and a product with features funded just-in-time by the customer!

Having customers order the just-in-time features or end users demonstrate a true business *necessity* for new software features requires you to have a development team that's nimble, responsive, and understands how to implement new systems with speed and agility.

Traditional projects with long life cycles—replete with elaborate high ceremony methodologies—just don't work. A nimble methodology which accommodates this rapid delivery of features is essential.

This brave new world of software development will consist of 90 day projects where the requirements change quickly. An entire software life cycle may be six weeks from start to finish. As soon as one release is done, you do another software development cycle.

Instead of calling it rapid application development, I've heard people call it "frantic application development!" It is challenging, but your rewards are features built-to-order, software built at less cost, with your company—and your career—as benefactors of this new model of success!

■ METHOD IN A NUTSHELL

Parts 2 through 5 of this book take you through the stages of every software project. In general, your 90 day project will look something like this:

- **Month 1**—Design UI. Parallel efforts like educating sales and marketing teams begin.

- **Month 2**—Create working demos and get initial feedback.

- **Month 3**—Production delivery of minimal but fully usable system. Find out what customers really like and need from the software.

The Four Phases

Web project methodologies are characterized by four distinct phases:

- **Analyze**—Analyze market; establish vision; determine long term products and features; prioritize requirements; select vendors and team.

- **Design**—Detail requirements; select platform and development tools; preliminary system and database design; creative design.

- **Develop**—Continued design, construct the system; change control; end user feedback on prototypes.
- **Deploy**—System in production.

An ongoing set of activities occurs to manage the project during each phase of the project life cycle.

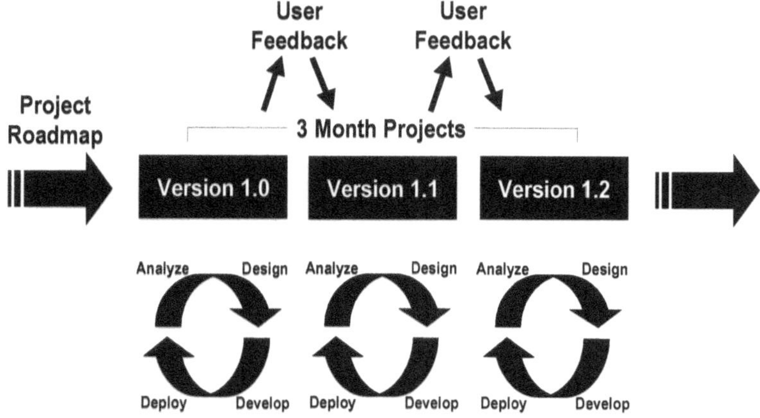

Series of Projects Lasting 3 Months or Less

Artifacts

The web project manager is responsible for the delivery and management of key project *artifacts* or deliverables. Artifacts are tangible elements produced during the project life cycle. They are outputs of various project activities including:

- **Models**
    1. Use-Cases
    2. Database Schema
- **Business Documents**
    1. Objective Statement
    2. Project Plan
    3. Budget
    4. Product Roadmap
- **System Components**
    1. HTML
    2. Custom Graphics
    3. Source Code

An effective web project manager ensures all project artifacts are archived appropriately, preferably under a change control system.

Don't Overdo It

Although I will spell out many things you may want to do within your project, by no means feel compelled to produce *all* of these artifacts within every project. If you find a particular deliverable unnecessary—don't do it. The following sections outline a list of management tools at your disposal. Don't feel obligated to use them all.

> ***When managing a project, choose the tools you need and get it done with speed!***

Chapter 2 Summary

Need for Speed

- Compressed business cycles demand projects must be completed faster—in Internet time.
- Projects should be no more than 30 to 90 days long.

Advantages of Web Speed

- Reduced 'ceremony.'
- Agility to adapt.
- Only essential features are built.
- Cost effective staffing model.

The Cost of Unneeded Features

- 50% to 80% of the lifetime cost of software is spent in maintenance mode.
- Unneeded features cost two to five times more than the initial development expense.

Built to Order Software

- Sub-90 day project timelines can be fine-tuned.
- New features should be delivered 'Just-In-Time'.
- Delivering systems in sub-90 days chunks allows you to react and 'fine-tune' the product roadmap.

Managing Software On Demand

- Roll out a small set of features in your initial release; deliver the rest "just-in-time."

Method in a Nutshell

- Web projects have four phases of activity: analyze, design, develop, and deploy.
- Standardized artifacts (project deliverables) are management tools necessary for project consistency.

Step 1

Analyze

Always bear in mind that your own resolution to
succeed is more important than any other.

— Abraham Lincoln

3

Successful Vision

Web projects, like any great undertaking, require planning and preparation. With the exception of business-to-business projects and internal projects, most web initiatives begin with analysis of market conditions. Do our customers really need this system? Is the ROI (return on investment) sufficient to justify this system?

■ MARKET ANALYSIS

Customers drive demand for web systems.

At the earliest stage, before the project is defined, high-level stakeholders conduct a survey of the market alternatives for the target end user. This is informally known as 'checking out the competition.'

Market Gaps take many forms:

- *Service levels not being offered at competitive prices.* By offering services to mass markets, economies of scale can provide cost savings that allow you to compete at lower prices.

- *Product features not being offered.* By adding new features to products or services you can beat the competition in cases where customer demand for new features is present.

- *Poor marketing to customers.* In many cases the products and services are present on the market, but are poorly marketed to customers. By understanding the profile of customers and the sales techniques needed you can outsell the competition.

In analyzing competitors look for such items as:

- What is the functionality of the web services offered?

- Are there other features or services customers demand not currently present in the marketplace?

- Does the web site appeal to the specific target customer?

- Are the pricing levels appropriate?

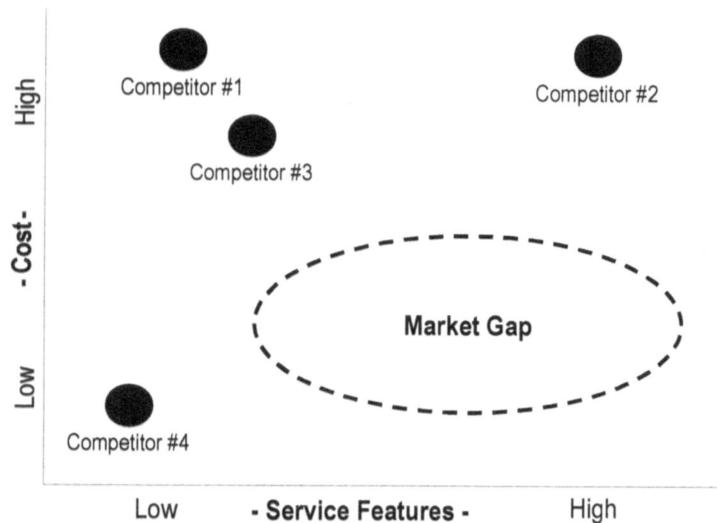

Identifying Market Gaps

Recognition of the market gaps then feeds into the development of a full-scale positioning strategy for your company's product rollout.

■ BUILD A BUSINESS CASE

A series of projects will be necessary to deliver a solution to address this market gap. The next step is to build a business case to justify the expense of implementing these projects. Examples of ways to justify these costs are:

- Increased productivity
- Ability to reach previously untouched customer segments
- Expected return on investment (ROI)

To back up the business case, it is necessary to have industry reports, case studies, market trends and other facts in place to support your premise.

■ PRODUCT ROADMAP

Once a market opportunity has been established, there is a business case for a series of new web projects. This is where the process of building a product roadmap begins.

The objective of the product roadmap is to lay out the envisioned long term products and features, even though only a *portion* of those services may be implemented in the near term.

The product roadmap serves as a guide to aid in areas such as:

- Architecture decisions
- Platform selection
- Database design

- Staffing

The product roadmap contains a forward thinking map of web systems being considered for delivery in the nine to eighteen month timeframe. Technologies and market conditions change with such rapidity that mapping out a product roadmap beyond 18 months is too speculative to have significant value.

You are not yet describing specific projects. You are focusing on 'big-picture' services to be offered, which will likely be broken down into several distinct web projects.

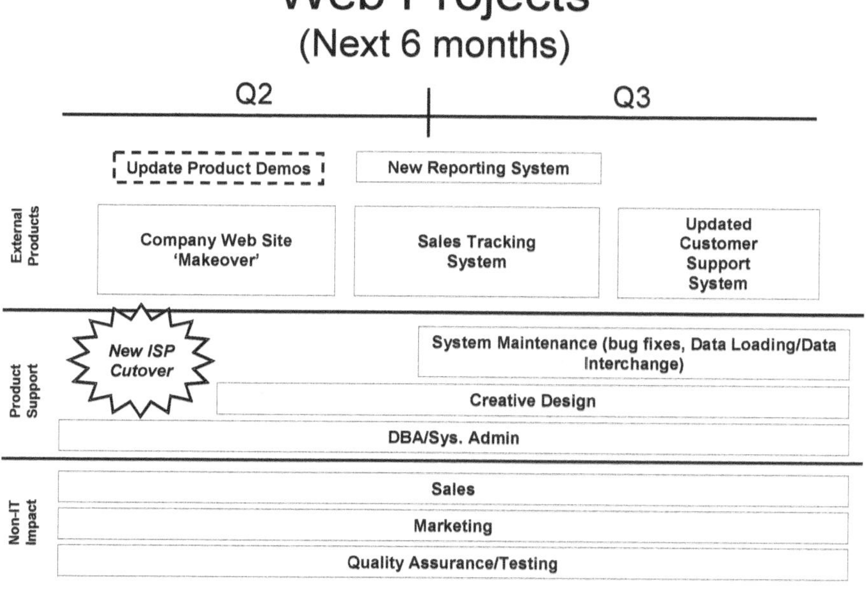

Product Roadmap

Discuss the product roadmap with key stakeholders and business leaders to get buy-in on the overall directions. This approval then allows you to develop and schedule specific web projects envisioned for the next six to nine months.

Why is a product roadmap so important? By having a roadmap that outlines current and future initiatives, you can understand the resources and technologies that you will need to bring to bear over the next many months. You will understand if your directions correctly align with the drivers of your business. Course corrections made early on are much less expensive than course corrections made deep into projects!

Educating web team members on future directions allows you to make design decisions to accommodate future features. For example, if you know an e-commerce module you are building does not require shipping and handling support in the initial phase, but this feature will likely be added within nine months, the developer can build the 'hooks' in the code to more easily allow the new feature to be coded in the future.

Likewise, to do appropriate database design which allows the schema to grow to support future features, having a long-term view of the product directions is imperative. Database designers require visibility to these future directions; otherwise the database schema will grow unwieldy over time and require costly structural changes.

Resource Dependencies

The final view in the product roadmap builds on the near term product roadmap and adds *resource dependencies*. An important aspect of this view is showing not only IT and creative design involvement, but also the involvement required from other groups such as:

- Vendors
- Marketing
- Sales
- Help Desk

This chart then serves as a catalyst for high-level discussions among business leaders to determine resource allocations.

Unlike other project management tools such as a detailed project plan, this diagram shows information at a large granularity. This is oriented to inform managers from disparate departments or companies who need to participate in the project planning process.

Failure to communicate effectively at this level often leads to misunderstanding between key project members. Many projects find only late in the development cycle, when a web site is almost ready to deploy, critical issues such as:

- Quality assurance test plans are not written and implemented, leaving code to languish in limbo for days or weeks.
- Marketing does not have ad copy prepared.
- Sales staff won't be able to sell until their staff are adequately training.

By presenting this high-level view of projects with their impact and rollout schedule, you have the opportunity to receive feedback from other department members about the project's impact to other areas of your company. You will obtain much needed feedback to feed into specific web project timelines and budgets.

■ OBJECTIVE STATEMENT

While market analysis and the product roadmap span long-term initiatives and multiple projects, the objective statement gives direction to a specific, sub-90 day web project. In order to achieve agreement between the business stakeholders on the objectives for the project, we must craft an objective statement.

Example Objective Statements

✔ "Implement a new, user-friendly accounting system to completely replace our current legacy accounting system."

✔ "Build a self-service support portal that will allow customers to solve 80% of technical questions without having to call our help desk."

✔ "Create a custom, built-from-scratch order entry system to provide custom, real-time product configuration."

The objective statement serves as a general answer to this question—"How will you know the project has been successfully completed?" It helps chart the course for your team so every project member knows in a nutshell what is the project goal.

The objective statement should be a brief paragraph, no more than half a page in length, describing the business objectives for the web project. These objectives must be tangible, measurable, and most of all, achievable.

During the entire life cycle of the project, the objective statement will serve as the pillar of stability in the sea of change. As tool selection, platform decision, vendor suggestions, feature requests and other change catalysts buffet the project, having a clear vision is imperative to stay focused on project goals.

Ask your team to *memorize* the objective statement. Give them a pop-quiz at team meetings. Drill it into their heads! Then ask your team to measure everything they do against the requirements of the objective statement.

Let us say a developer has realized there is a more elegant way to write a section of code which is already completed and ready for beta testing. This new innovation will allow greater flexibility should the company decide later to localize the code to allow for foreign languages and other currencies. "It will only take two or three days to re-write it," they beg.

Now is the time to whip out the objective statement and with draconian ruthlessness evaluate the value of this suggestion. Does it support the objective statement? If the answer is 'no', then decline the developer's request—and meet your deadline.

Conversely, a nebulous objective statement, or worse of all, having no objective statement at all, will lead to a nebulous outcome. Have specific objectives and keep reminding yourself and your team of them.

Chapter 3 Summary

Market Analysis

- Identify market gaps and develop a full-scale positioning strategy.

Business Case

- Create a business case to cost justify the project initiatives.

Product Roadmap

- Create a product roadmap of the near term IT initiatives.

- Use to educate business leaders and web team members on key directions of the business.

Resource Dependencies

- Serves as a catalyst for high-level discussions between business leaders to determine resource allocations.

Objective Statement

- While market analysis and the product roadmap span long-term initiatives and multiple projects, the objective statement gives direction to a specific, sub-90 day web project.

- Consists of a brief paragraph, no more than half a page in length.

- Describes the business objectives for the web project.

4

Decisive Directions

Now that we have our product roadmap and our objective statement for this specific project, our next step is to identify the requirements for the first phase rollout of the web system.

■ DEFINE REQUIREMENTS

Develop the Candidate Features List

Schedule a meeting or series of meetings and use brainstorming techniques to produce a list of candidate features. I have sometimes heard this list called 'ramblings' because at this stage the list is not structured or prioritized. This candidate features list is a document with bulleted system features, each item being a short sentence or two description to be fleshed out in later meetings.

Prioritizing Phase I Features

The next (and arguably hardest) phase is prioritization. Immediately subsequent to the brainstorming session where the requirements list is identified, schedule time to prioritize each item in the candidate features list. One effective way to do the prioritization is to assign a priority level of A, B or C, defined as follows:

- **'A' Priority**
  Absolutely 'must have' features essential to make the system viable. Without this feature the system cannot even function.

- **'B' Priority**
  This feature is critical and needed within three to nine months, but the system can function without the feature for a short time.

- **'C' Priority**
  This feature is a 'Nice to have' feature. This feature is needed eventually but not necessarily in the next three to six months.

After the prioritization meeting, each candidate feature has either an A, B, or C priority assigned to it. The 'A' features serve as the working Phase I requirements list.

Develop a Working Estimate

The next item of business is to create a working estimate —a rough time and cost projection of Phase I features used for planning purposes. The web project manager working with the key technical personnel who will be responsible for implementing the project creates this.

You will often encounter a culture shock if you are working with developers who are not familiar with this methodology. This is with good reason. In one sense we have the 'cart before the horse' here—we are doing time and cost estimates *without* having detailed design, a violation of a cardinal rule of methodologies architected for longer traditional project cycles. Two factors make 'working' estimates possible at this early stage:

- Stress that it is an estimate only, and that the estimate will be revised after completing design.

- By having the project contain only those features which can be coded in fewer than 90 days, we have a more manageable set of features easily estimated by 'gut feel' than the larger six to nine month or longer projects.

After reviewing the Phase I features and arriving at a preliminary estimate from key technical personnel, you can then develop a simple budget and timeline—usually with a simple spreadsheet or project management tool

The key driving principle of web projects is managing projects within cycles of three months or less. You can juggle with adding or deleting features to be included in Phase I and you can map out different models of how much money you will be willing to spend to deliver the project—but one immutable principle is the *calendar*. Don't let the project take more than three months! If you end up with a five-month project, break it into two three month projects instead.

You may be wondering about the math on this. By breaking it into two projects (Phase I and Phase II) each cycle must have it's own QA and release process. Splitting up the project takes longer than one mammoth five month project. Ironically though, it costs less in the long run due to principles already discussed, such as a flat lined staffing model and delivering a system more closely aligned to true market demand.

One of the keys to doing a three-month project is doing a few short iterations of these tasks:

- Prioritization

- High-level design

- Project level of effort

- Timeline cost estimation

After you have done a first pass at these tasks, reconvene with key stakeholders to tweak the 'A' priority items.

If the cost or timeline seems out of order, then you must go back and trim Phase I features with the involvement and approval of project stakeholders. Make sure to stress that Phase I features must be those features which absolutely *must* be present to make the system function.

Remember the Time/Quality/Cost triangle. If you change any one leg of the triangle, there is an immediate effect on the other legs of the triangle that must be balanced.

For example, if you determine the features exceed what the existing company staff can implement within three months, then you have the option of adding consultants to increase project resources—which drives up cost.

Likewise, if you decide to not increase your resource level due to budget constraints, and that none of the features can be removed, then you are forced to implement the features in a 'quick and dirty' fashion. You then see the quality factor go down. In some cases this is acceptable; for example the project is only needed for demo purposes. If you need a proof of concept for further funding, this mode of development is appropriate.

Continue iterating between estimates and revisions of requirements until you arrive at an acceptable balance of features and cost to deliver the project in less than ninety days.

Managing Expectations

After cutting product features down to inside the three-month project window, the next most difficult aspect of requirements definition is managing expectations.

It is imperative to make stakeholders who participated in the requirements definition not feel like their input will be lost. When you cut features out, make sure they are well documented and place project artifacts in a shared location available to the participants of the prioritization process.

By tracking and sharing this information we emphasize that by cutting the requirement from the Phase I rollout, we are *not* saying a feature will not ever be delivered. We are simply saying it will not be in the Phase I delivery.

■ CONCEPTUAL UI

Even before the requirement prioritization is completed development can begin on the conceptual UI (user interface). The conceptual user interface is the initial foray into the creative design for your web solution.

If the web project is an internal system the look and feel experience for the end user is not nearly as critical as a B2B (business to business) or B2C (business to consumer) solution. In all cases you will find user acceptance of a web site is greatly enhanced when appropriate attention is paid to look and feel.

With established businesses you are often able to leverage existing branding and graphic guidelines. With new web initiatives a creative design team must put together two or three prototypes for management approval.

The sample design at this stage is purely conceptual. The design is a hasty mockup designed to achieve consensus on:

- Common tool bars
- Role-specific navigational schemes
- Overall look and feel of the site

If the system is a consumer-oriented solution, have two or three designs put together. Each conceptual mockup will consist of typically one to five screens demonstrating the key elements of a particular design.

Functionality will direct the form and design of the interface. Consumer oriented sites may require a near-zero wait time for graphical elements and have special attention paid to optimize the number of clickthroughs. Internal sites may be more oriented toward quick access of business applications.

In all cases attention should be paid to good design techniques. Users should always know:

- Where they are
- Where they can go from the current page
- What they will find when they click

The key goal is to get buy-in on the overall look and feel. At this stage, not every individual page is laid out. More attention will be paid to the detailed user interface layout during the design phase, when a visual site map will be constructed.

■ ARCHITECTURE

One key decision which will factor into the final project plan is identifying a *candidate* architecture. It is called a candidate architecture at this point since the later design phase will validate our planning assumptions. Later we will learn how results from testing the base architecture may in fact change our architecture assumptions.

Fortunately, the Internet has matured to the point where many 'off-the-shelf' architectures exist which have been used over and over again successfully by many companies. Selecting one of these 'canned' architectures is sufficient to meet the requirements of the majority of web projects.

Often the architecture selection comes down to a simple matter of platform bias. The good news is that multiple off-the-shelf architectures have been used successfully to deliver mission critical, scalable systems.

Tales from the Trenches

The conference call didn't go well at all.

I was consulting with a large company on the largest web project in which I had ever participated. Over 250 people were working on one large, massive re-engineering project to convert a legacy system that ran all of the company's backend systems to a new, re-engineered system that moved all applications to a web architecture.

The only problem was, the application server we were depending on wasn't working. The phone call had just confirmed the bug existed.

We had spent $2.5 million on a contract with a major application server vendor to buy the best support package available. Months into the project, we ran into a serious architectural flaw that was preventing us from integrating several pieces of our core systems together. I had finally isolated it to a CORBA bug in the back processing system.

I told one of the VPs,"We can't work around this. We have about 75 developers sitting around with nothing to do until we can solve this problem."

> *The application server vendor acknowledged the system flaw, but would not commit to issuing a release to fix the problem for a minimum of 6 months.*
>
> *A $2.5 million investment didn't buy us a fix when we needed it. 75 developers sitting idle and hundreds of thousands of dollars of code written that couldn't be integrated together.*
>
> *What if we had used open source products instead? We could have spent a few thousand dollars on customizing Open Source software for our needs. When an issue like this arose, we'd have the source and could fix it.*
>
> *Since then, I've used Open Source software whenever possible, even if I have to pay to customize it. I don't want to be a victimized by an unresponsive, closed source vendor ever again!*

Other considerations in architecture selection:

- Is the server scalable enough to match anticipated customer volumes? What are the uptime requirements: 99%, 99.9% or 99.999%?

- What are the data integrity requirements? Will data replication and a hot backup be a requirement or is a cold backup with some minimal data loss acceptable?

- Does your internal staff have the skills to successfully manage the environment, or does it make more sense to farm management of the system out to an enterprise service provider?

In most cases you don't have time to build out a huge, massively scalable architecture. Instead, deploy an initial system on one of these canned architectures and migrate to a more ideal system once customer volumes have validated the additional expense.

Chapter 4 Summary

Define Requirements

- Identify a candidate features list that is not prioritized.
- Prioritize Phase I features.
- Develop a working estimate.
- Iteratively work to balance features and budget until you have a rough project estimate.
- Projects must be delivered in three months or less.
- Manage expectations by retaining B and C priority items in a shared location to be reviewed in future phases.

Conceptual UI

- Create multiple conceptual mockups.
- Achieve buy-in on the overall look and feel.

Architecture

- Identify a candidate architecture based on an 'off-the-shelf' proven solution.

5

Power by Partnering

In the planning stage of a project an up-front business decision needs to be made—do you build your system from scratch and own all rights, or do you license a preexisting application from a third party vendor?

■ BUILD VS. BUY

Usually systems are complex enough that the real question is not *whether* to build vs. buy, but rather *which parts* of the system to build and which parts should be purchased off-the-shelf or outsourced to application service providers.

If your project is sizable, the inevitable outcome is that some vendors will be involved in your Internet system. Part of determining the success of your project is making good decisions about when to outsource, what service providers to use, and making sure you manage your vendors properly.

Benefits of Packaged Solutions

There are many factors which make a pre-packaged solution attractive.

Attracting and retaining a quality staff to implement and support the system can be costly.

A limited budget usually means your system will have only limited functionality. Pre-packaged solutions often have rich feature sets.

With pre-packed solutions you have a drastically faster time to market. Factoring in the opportunity cost (the cost of passing up one investment in favor of another) of delaying a system's implementation for months or years often shows that even the costliest vendor solutions may save the company money in the long run.

Probably the most overlooked benefits are the cost of ownership. The cost to initially develop a software solution is typically only 20% of the total cost of the solution. 80% of cost is expended during the maintenance phase as the software is upgraded and new features are added. During each new release, even minor releases, all the familiar software development life cycle costs such as testing and system administration are incurred. So a packaged solution may be more expensive than the construction cost of building the solution yourself, but don't forget the total cost of ownership over the life of the system.

> *An 80% solution in three months is better than a 100% solution in three years.*

Buyer Beware

Buying a packaged solution is not without issues. You do give up the level of control you have with an in-house solution. You usually lose the ability to completely customize the system.

Giving up control and access to the core technology of the system in many cases does not meet the business objectives of the project.

Packaged software solutions are good if the business process model in the software matches your business rules exactly. Many times this is not the case, and you end up changing your business processes to match the constraints of the software solution. What is quick and clean on the technical side is often messy and disruptive on the business side.

The cost of numerous changes and adjustments and unintended consequences from changing your business processes to match the way the software works can lead to unexpected cost overruns. Be sure to incorporate such contingencies into your build-vs.-buy decision.

■ THE ASP SOLUTION

Many packaged solutions require you to buy or rent the software but install, configure, and maintain the software on your own servers.

A variation of the packaged 'shrink wrap' solution is the application service provider (ASP) model. ASPs exist providing almost every imaginable service offered: data storage, supply-chain integration, business intelligence functions and many other specialized business services.

Benefits

Hosting part of your system with an ASP has several advantages. An application service provider is responsible for maintaining and updating the software—freeing up your money and resources to concentrate on other things.

ASPs possess economies of scale. This means the ASP will likely provide a service more inexpensively than you could implement it yourself.

There is also an advantage to the cost model of using ASPs. Building a solution entirely from scratch means paying for an entire system up front. Buying a packed solution often means significant cash outlay even when the software is amortized over multiple years. The ASP model typically allows for a minimum up front fee, with the bulk of the cost coming through monthly payments, often in a metered, usage-based fee model. This significantly reduces up front costs. It also reduces risks, as you are not locked into a solution for several years. You should constantly evaluate best-of-breed ASP solutions and switch vendors when it makes business sense.

Selecting an ASP

When you select a best-in-class ASP to serve as your vendor, you are entering into a partnership which will be critical to the success of your system.

Probably the greatest risk is that the ASP will not stay in business. Find out if the ASP is publicly held and if it is profitable. If it is privately held it may not disclose its financials. In this case, evaluate its business model—is it profitable or likely to be so? You can ask about the pricing model and do the math to determine it's fiscal soundness.

Ask for references. If possible, contact two or more reference customers and see if they have been satisfied with their service.

What if you were to use an ASP and it goes out of business? Understand what happens to your data and servers should the ASP fail. Develop a contingency plan to deal with such possibilities. Make sure there are clauses in your vendor agreement to deal with such possibilities. One often overlooked clause is to require the vendor to put the software into escrow in case it is purchased and the source code be made available to existing customers for them to access, own and develop going forward.

Avoid long-term contracts. One-year contracts are usually the longest you should sign. Make sure you have an 'out clause' should the service level decline. Re-evaluate alternatives to the vendor every six to twelve months. As contracts come up for renewal you can switch vendors, or at the very least use information on competitors to help negotiate better contract renewals with your current provider.

Tales from the Trenches

The DoS attack hit, and it hit us hard.

Denial of Service attacks are nothing new, but my company's agreement with our hosting service provider said they use BGP technology to route our web traffic to other provider networks in case of such attacks.

They oversold their capabilities, and our company-critical web site was down for almost two hours. Worse yet, their support desk tried to act like nothing had happened. Our monitoring software running remotely told us otherwise.

> *We complained; they equivocated. They said it wouldn't happen again. We didn't trust them, and made contingency plans.*
>
> *We got hit again by another DoS attack, and that's when we threw in the towel.*
>
> *We executed our contingency plan, and within three days we had all of our systems (multiple servers, databases and web software) converted to a rival hosting service provider.*
>
> *Having a backup vendor, a contingency plan, and an agreement that contains an out clause gave us the protection we needed to keep our customers' systems up and running.*

Service-Level Agreements

A well-written service-level agreement (SLA) is critical to dealing with ASPs, ISPs and other outsourced vendors. The SLA defines the critical points of the relationship between your company and the vendor by stating:

- **Responsibilities of Each Party**—What are the specific responsibilities of your company versus the responsibilities of the service provider? It is often helpful to stipulate a specific line of demarcation when division of responsibilities are unclear. For example, when co-locating a company owned server at an ISP, you might identify the line of demarcation of responsibility as: "The ISP responsibility ends at the network card (NIC) —all server hardware and software is the sole responsibility of the customer."

- **Availability**—Does the service need to be available on a 24x7 basis? If so, there inevitably will be the need for scheduled downtime to conduct routine maintenance. You need to understand the vendor's policy regarding time windows in which maintenance is routinely performed, the maximum outage that shall be incurred, and how much notice you as a customer can expect to receive of such changes.

- **Scalability**—What sort of scalability ceilings can you expect from the vendor? What performance or throughput can you expect, and at what point would this degrade? What is the cost and timeframe to add more capacity to your service should scalability or performance become an issue?

- **Security**—Exposing part of your business process and data to a third party vendor obligates the vendor to meet the security requirements appropriate to your business. What guarantees or policies does the vendor have to keep your data protected and private?

- **API Stability**—This is the most overlooked aspect of SLAs. In cases where the vendor is an ASP that has an application programming interface (API) which your system is coded to communicate with, it is vital the vendor honor these specifications. Any API will evolve, but you want to work out—in advance of a signed contract—your expectations. If an API does change, how long will the old APIs be recognized and work? How much notice will you receive of such changes? Many vendors will balk about putting such guarantees in writing. My advice is to have conversations with personnel at high levels at the vendor to emphasize the importance and sensitivity of this need.

- **Remediation**—Should the vendor fail to meet the terms of the SLA, what sort of remediation will you receive? The more 'teeth' the remediation clause of an SLA has the more you can expect to pay for the service. Be prepared to pay a premium if you want the highest guaranteed availability and scalability from your vendor.

- **Out Clause**—Having a good out clause is even more important than the remediation clause. If the vendor's service does not meet expectation, make sure you can drop the vendor, even if you've signed a contract for 12 months of service.

Quality SLAs can be difficult and costly to negotiate. Evaluate the business requirements of your Internet system to determine just what service is absolutely required. Balance this with the cost of such services.

Line up alternate vendors to provide continuity to the vendor's service. Even if the vendor isn't going out of business, if the service level declines dramatically you need to be able to quickly transfer to another vendor rather than spend weeks fighting with unacceptable service.

■ PROFESSIONAL SERVICES

In addition to using packaged software and outsourced ASP solutions, you may also need to leverage personnel from a professional services firm to staff your project.

Staff Supplementation

The simplest consultant scenario is staff supplementation. You provide oversight and manage the consultant along with other team members. The consultant is typically paid by the hour.

One key to finding good consultants is the same as with successful permanent hires: a thorough interview and screening. Check out the consultant's resumé, call their references, and perform a technical assessment of their skills.

Many consulting firms allow you to 'evaluate' the consultant for a few days. If their performance or skills are not acceptable you can 'reject' them and get someone else to take their place, often without having to pay for the wasted time. Discuss this possibility in advance with the consulting firm with which you are engaging.

Project Based Consulting

Use only larger and more established consulting firms when outsourcing entire projects. In these cases you are relying on the professional services firm to run the project. The consulting firm takes full responsibility for deadlines and cost overruns. This comes at a premium cost, but also greatly reduces your risk, which will save you money in the long run.

Investigate fixed fee and fixed time options when they make good business sense as a means to ensure time to market.

Selecting a Professional Services Firm

To select your professional services vendor, first create a short list of potential vendors. Assess each vendor's background, including experience and project history.

Determine if the services firm is suitably capitalized. A publicly held company will have financials available for public review.

Some service firms have a vertical focus in a technology or market that may add value to their services if you need a specific skill set.

Be wary of consulting firms without a demonstrable project track record. Ask for case studies and references—and do not be afraid to call and check them out.

For full-scale project management firms, you will also need to analyze the professional services firm's methodology. A rigorous methodology to manage the software development process means less risk to you as a customer.

Examine closely the change management process proposed by the consulting firm. The requirements of your project will undoubtedly change with time. An experienced consulting firm should provide structured change control mechanisms to allow you to alter the project features, even if it means increased cost.

Lastly, before any consulting arrangement takes place, make sure you have a professional services agreement in place. This is a legal document stipulating the rules by which both you the client and the consulting firm agree to do business. This protects the vendor from someone hiring away their consultants without remuneration, and protects your intellectual properties and proprietary information. You will also want to include a provision stipulating that the consulting firm cannot also hire away *your* talent.

■ THE RFP PROCESS

When you plan to outsource an entire project, it is often useful to use a request for proposal (RFP). The RFP is a standardized requirements document giving enough information to a consulting firm to provide you with an initial bid. This allows you to get several consulting firms to give you estimates on their fee to provide a solution. This gives you a comparison of project management approaches, architectural solutions and costs.

RFP Structure

Items that should be included in any RFP:

- **Business Goal Definition**—The mission statement of your company.

- **Market Definition**—List of competitors and your target audience.

- **Current Systems Overview**—Explanation of existing systems and architecture (if any) to be integrated into the project.

- **Preference for Site Architecture**—If you have a set of technologies or preferred vendors in mind, state this in your RFP.

- **Hosting**—Who will host and monitor the system.

- **Scaling Requirements**—The scalability requirements for near and long term needs.

- **Firewall and Security**—Security requirements for the system.

- **Ongoing Maintenance**—After the project is over, who is responsible for maintaining the system? If it is you, make sure you specify cross-training is needed to do a knowledge transfer to your internal staff.

- **Internal and External Team Responsibilities**—Delineate clearly between the client's responsibilities versus the consulting team's responsibilities.

- **Design Specifications**—Even early in the project life cycle you undoubtedly have some preliminary designs captured. Make sure these are included to give the vendor a feel for the project scope.

- **Time Line and Budget**—Set realistic expectations about any aggressive timelines or budgetary constraints. You do not want to tip your hand as to your specific budget, but by setting the tone you weed out vendors who are not good fits to meet your project constraints.

RFP Responses

Engaging in an RFP process and trying to deliver systems in web speed is almost an oxymoron. There is a way, however, to incorporate the RFP process into your project life cycle and still deliver your system in a timely manner.

The key is to compress the time frame for the RFP process into weeks not months.

After creating the RFP, distribute it to your short list of possible vendors. You should allow time for vendors to ask questions and for you to give responses to the soliciting companies.

On-site visits to the prospective vendor's offices can qualify the capabilities of a prospective vendor, as well as other intangibles such as their professionalism, office moral and other factors.

Allow a reasonable time period for internal review of RFP responses. The responses will be proposals from the prospective solutions providers.

After making your vender decision, all vendors should be notified of final selection. It is courteous to share feedback with non-selected vendors about their relative strengths and weaknesses so they learn from the experience and not have a total loss for the often considerable effort they have spent understanding your business need.

Vendor Management

Given that outsourcing is a strategic part of much IT systems delivery, many IT managers spend 50% or more of their time managing vendors. Vendors are resources that are an extension to your internal personnel. Selecting the right vendor and putting the right management controls in place is a key part of your project success.

Chapter 5 Summary

The ASP Solution

- Application Service Providers (ASPs) can maintain and update software, freeing up your money and re- sources, and are often cheaper due to economies of scale.

- Check references and make contingency plans when doing business with ASPs.

- Obtain Service Level Agreements (SLAs) from out- sourced vendors that include an out clause.

Professional Services

- With staff supplementation you provide the project management and oversight, and save money.

- Use only larger and more established consulting firms when outsourcing entire projects.

- Have a Professional Services Agreement in place with any consultants with whom you do business.

The RFP Process

- When you plan to outsource an entire project, use a Request For Proposal (RFP). The RFP is a standardized requirements document giving enough information to a consulting firm to provide you with an initial bid.

- Make sure to include enough information in your RFP for the vendors to give an adequate response.

- The time frame for the total RFP process should be weeks not months.

6

On Time, On Budget

To make projects come in on time, under budget, act like a consultant even if you're not one. Make your bottom line shine by utilizing these proven secrets of project management success!

Through years of consulting, I've learned to focus on client expectations—how are we doing on our budget and schedule? There is a signed contract, and your credibility as a consultant is riding on the success of this project. Depending on your relationship with your consulting firm, whether you make money or lose money may even affect your paycheck. With these incentives you tend to pay a lot of attention to detail—your livelihood depends on it!

Even when you're not a consultant (for example, you're working within a corporate setting and it's an internally funded project), treating the project as if you were a consultant, as if it were a fixed-fee project with a definite time-boxed deadline and a finite budget, will give you better control. To manage your projects properly, give them that sense of purpose and urgency as if you were an outside consultant.

■ PUT THE LID ON COST OVERRUNS

How do you define what those initial 20 percent of features are that you're really going to build, versus the 80 percent of feature requests that you reserve for your just-in-time, on demand, build-to-order list?

Simple—use lethal prioritization! Ask these questions. Will it kill the project not to have this feature? Will the product not work if this feature is not included? Can you do a functional demo for an end-user without it?

If you can't even demo the system without a feature, then obviously it's a core requirement that needs to be included. Eliminating anything not absolutely required is what lethal prioritization is all about.

Focus on developing the most important features. Help the end user focus on what their people are willing to pay for instead of what they simply find interesting or think is neat.

Align the scope of the project with your time constraints and available resources. As a general rule of thumb, don't implement a project longer than three months in duration. If you have six months worth of features to develop, version one needs to be a three-month project delivering only a small, core feature set. After it rolls out, see what the end users are really using, and *then* start working on the second set of features.

Before you get too far in the next iteration of product development, you'll be getting invaluable feedback from the first release. Once software is in use, you'll get feedback on what they *really* need to do their job.

One of the nice things about the web is having a high degree of visibility to end user's activity. You can see web pages people access, what paths they take to the system, and what features are actually touched. You can place links to "coming soon" pages in as hooks so you can see if anyone would use this feature if it were there. And if they don't even *try* to access the feature, you'll have a pretty good idea it is not needed.

It is helpful to have an automated feature request tracking system. Encourage users to email in their request, and route and track these feature requests in a database. At the start of each release cycle, review the feature requests. If a feature was only asked for once or twice, it may not be something worth building!

When you do projects back-to-back in three month cycles, you gain early and concrete visibility to what your customers *really* want—what is really needed in the marketplace. This gives you the strategic advantage to succeed. Put a lid on cost overruns—use lethal prioritization to "right-size" your project.

■ SPEAK THE SAME LANGUAGE

There are three terms every web project manager should know and use: 'Happy days,' 'LOE,' and 'COB.'

Happy Days

No, not the TV series with Fonzie.

Let's say you're talking to your developers and asking them for an estimate. Someone says, "It will take three days to do this certain task." What do those three days mean?

Is this a day and a half's worth of real work they've already padded by an extra day and a half to account for unexpected snags? Or is that three days of work if things are *ideal* and they don't get distracted and they don't run into any snags with the code? In which case this number may be unrealistically low. Things often do not work out perfectly in the real world.

Let's think about the (sometimes rare) days you don't run into any particular snags and everything is going well on your project. There are few distractions. The technology works like you expect it to. These are what I call 'happy days.'

When a developer gives me a quote, I always ask him to give me a 'happy day' estimate. In this way, every developer gives me a common baseline estimate based on a consistent, optimistic notion. Then I can take these well-understood estimates and come back and pad it by 25 percent or 50 percent or 100 percent, depending on the risk factors of the project.

Tales from the Trenches

I was in New York working with a local project manager to wrap up a proposal for a fairly large project integrating a new e-commerce site to a backend mainframe system.

I reviewed the project plan, then asked, "How much padding is in this project?"

The local project manager who had compiled the estimate replied defensively, "Well, the developers already padded their numbers before I added up the totals."

"Oh, how <u>much</u> did they pad their estimates? And are you sure all the developers did in fact pad their estimates? And did they all use this padding factor?"

> *Though a little flustered at first, the project manager worked with me and we discovered the 'padding' the developers had created ranged from no padding at all to a padding of 20%. As it was, when we reworked the projections using 'Happy Day' estimates from the developers, and applying a uniform 25% pad at the end, we ended up with a truly accurate number that was tens of thousands of dollars more than initially thought.*
>
> *Use consistent language and methods to create your estimates!*

LOE

LOE stands for 'Level of Effort.' LOE means how many days of *work* will it take. Not calendar days, but days of effort. Know the difference between effort (work) and duration. Work and effort are synonyms—how many hours will it take an individual developer to code this particular task? This is often dramatically different from calendar time. A two week LOE project will take over a month calendar time to complete if you have vacation, holidays or other distractions competing with your availability to work on the project.

In general your calendar delivery time is going to be longer than your total work time. Make sure you make this clear to your stakeholders when you deliver an estimate of how long the project will take. LOE is different from how long it will take for the project to be completed!

COB

Another acronym which will help give you a baseline for a common language with your teammates and other people you work with is 'COB'—close of business.

When you're on projects delivered in compressed time cycles, it's really critical you nail down the delivery date within *a matter of days*, sometimes even a specific day. Make sure when you say, "It's going to be available on the 15th," to specify *close of business* on the 15th. That means it is delivered at the end of the business day.

Come 8:00 a.m. on the 15th, when your CEO shows up and says, "Hey, when's the software going to be available for me to preview," you can point back to your e-mail you sent them and say, "It's close of business on the 15th." Clear up misunderstandings before they start, and you will spare yourself the headache of dealing with misplaced expectations.

■ USE THE 1.25/1.5/2.0 RULE

Project plans should be detailed down to the nearest half-day. Don't estimate down to the hour and get bogged down into minutiae! This is overkill. Estimates rounded to four hour and eight hour increments provide enough detail for working estimates, without bothering to try an catalog the hundreds of one and two hour tasks. Just make sure your rounded estimate factors in time for all these various tasks!

Draw from your own past experience in making estimates. Talk to people skilled in the technology you're going to use. They will give invaluable feedback to how long *they* think it takes to implement the various project components.

Generally, that gut feel estimate is going to be fairly accurate if you have experienced people evaluating the requirements.

When you have the initial rough project plan completed and have put together a 'happy day' estimate, you are ready to apply padding. Things can and do go wrong; it is your job to plan for them!

How much you pad is going to depend on how risky the project is. That's where the 1.25/1.5/2.0 rule comes in.

Straightforward Projects (25% Pad)

Projects which involve a set of tasks you're familiar with —something you've done before in another setting—generally should be padded by 25 percent. Take your baseline 'happy day' estimate and multiply by 1.25 to get the final, padded estimate.

Projects with Risk Factors (50% Pad)

All projects involve some amount of risk, but some are riskier than others. Perhaps one of the team members is new (and inexperienced), or you're changing platforms in the middle of the project (try to avoid this!) or there are other factors making you question your capability to deliver.

In these cases, multiple by 1.5 and give yourself a 50 percent buffer.

Cutting Edge Projects (100% Pad)

Many projects involve one or more cutting edge technologies. Any time you introduce a brand-new software platform, integration with a vendor you've never interfaced with before, or an unproven, cutting edge new technology, unforeseen problems may arise which cause a change in technology mid-project.

Multiply these estimates by 2.0. Will the scope of your project really come in *double* your original estimate? It well may. It's better to under-promise and over-deliver than to over-promise and find yourself branded as the manager who couldn't deliver the project on time, on budget.

Avoid implementing system upgrades or other seemingly minor system configuration changes as part of a new custom software release. Break system or platform changes out as a separate project.

If at all possible, negotiate to break off the adoption of a new platform or technology into a separate project altogether. Put together a pilot program which implements the new technology, and run this before, after or even in parallel with your actual *software development* project.

Whenever possible, reduce the variables in your project by excluding such changes as new platform adoption.

■ OUT OF THE BALLPARK ESTIMATES

Another secret of bringing projects in on time, under budget is to make sure any initial 'rough' estimates you give are *out of the ballpark*.

Before you do a formal estimate, after you've done a little bit of research and you've put together a project plan with specific timelines, before the project even gets approved—the stakeholders are likely to ask—"Well, what's a ballpark estimate for how long it would take to build this project?"

They're going to want an estimate as early as possible, and rightly so. If you know the project will cost between $500,000 and $1,000,000 to build, and the company has only budgeted $100,000 for the project, then you have a show-stopper early on. This is obviously important for managers to know.

It's inevitable you'll have to deliver ballpark estimates—business reality demands it. Given this, make sure your ballpark estimate really has a broad range to it and the upper range is significantly padded. Regardless of how many disclaimers you add, the customer is going to remember what you told them—and they will hold you to it! So make sure you have a broad range with sufficient breathing room. You may well be the one to manage this project and expectations will be for you to be within this early budget quote.

In general, ball park estimates are fairly accurate for sub-three-month projects. As a rule of thumb, the range for a ballpark estimate is minus 25, plus 75 percent of your initial shoot-from-the-hip guess. If you haven't done design, it is a ballpark guess, and so I generally will stress it *could* be between this range—it is not a firm estimate.

For example, if I guess it to be a $100,000 project, I would say, "I estimate this project could cost between $75,000 and $175,000." This is a number accurate enough to do budgeting and make business decisions about continuing—or canceling—the project.

Make sure you give yourself a significant buffer so they can't pin you to an arbitrary number that was not intended to be a firm estimate!

■ DON'T GIVE IN TO BROWBEATING

The first quote you give your customer—the one that makes the client gasp—is inevitably the right one.

Of course, they're going to come back and challenge you. "Surely it wouldn't take that long!" they'll say. And the non-technical person will try to describe to you why it wouldn't take so long and cost so much money. But don't give in to browbeating. Don't give into the pressure the manager or CEO is going to give you. The cost is what it is.

Whenever they start applying pressure to you, as often will happen, produce and use the oft quoted Time/Quality/Cost triangle.

The Time/Quality/Cost triangle is like a three legged stool. Change one leg and you will affect the balance of the project triangle.

If you decrease the cost of a project, you will have to reduce the features (quality) you deliver, or radically increase the timeline in which you deliver the project. If you increase the scope of the project, you will have to take longer or spend more to deliver it. If you decrease the time in which you deliver a large project, the cost will go up, or the quality will go down, or both.

And, of course, some timelines cannot be realistically reduced. You can't use nine women to have a baby in one month, after all!

People have to make choices. If they don't want to pay as much money, then either the schedule will have to change or the features will have to be reduced.

Whenever one leg of the triangle gets affected, you'll have to adjust one of the other two legs of the triangle to bring things back into balance.

When people ask for new features, don't say 'no'; rather, give people their options. "Well, we *can* do everything you want, but it's going to cost more. If you don't want to pay as much, we can take out some features. We can do what you want at this reduced price, but it may take nine or 18 months because we'll have to just work it in when we can around other higher priority projects."

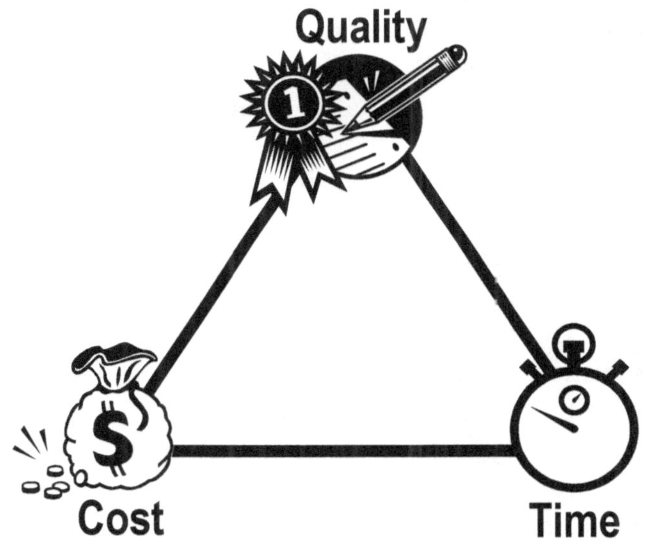

Time/Quality/Cost Triangle

Draw your Time/Quality/Cost triangle on the whiteboard, work with your stakeholders to align the project with the business needs, but do not give in to browbeating!

■ BE REALISTIC ABOUT UTILIZATION

You can have the perfect estimate, an accurate project plan, and the best team of developers on the planet, but still miss your project deadline by several weeks if you aren't realistic about utilization.

What is utilization? Utilization is the amount of work you're *really* going to get out of people. People aren't always available. People are going to need time off. Take this into account when you formulate your project timeline.

In general, a fully available team working full time on your project is still only available about 80 percent of the time. They're going to have meetings and other distractions. They'll have vacation days, sick days, and holidays. Generally, over a three-month period of time, you're going to only have 80 percent of the hours worked in normal business weeks actually being applied to working on your project.

Account for the possibility of developer turnover. If a key project team member leaves your company to take another job, this will obviously have a significant impact on your project deadline. If you have a flight risk on your team, or if you are working on a project whose deadline is absolutely immovable, consider the possibility of turnover and how you would deal with it.

It's helpful if you get people's vacation schedules in advance, and with short projects you usually are able to do this. Don't craft a project plan where someone calling in sick with a cold for two days causes your delivery date to slip!

Look at the holiday schedule, and find out the personal schedules of your team members ("get your time off requests for the next three months in now!") and put an appropriate buffer into your timeline to account for utilization.

■ GET BUY-IN FROM PARTICIPANTS

One of the fastest paths to failure is having a project manager dream up a project cost and schedule without the feedback of the people that will implement it. Nothing is more dismaying than being handed a project plan doomed for failure from the start—a five-month project that you're asked to deliver in two months.

Don't create estimates which do not have buy-in from the participants. Always make sure the people who are going to be *working* on the project are the people giving feedback into the project estimate.

Involve the team members who will participate in the project—get their buy-in by having them review and approve the project plan that's going to be carried out.

Even if you're an experienced project manager, it's helpful to have the other people double-check your numbers. It's best not to rely on just one person, but have the estimates reviewed by at least a couple of sets of eyes. This ensures your estimates are accurate. And if the project runs into difficulties because of a bad estimate, your team members will be less likely to hold it against you, if they themselves approved the estimate to which you are now accountable.

■ NO QUOTES WITHOUT BLUEPRINTS

Before a project has been approved, while it's still in the conception stage, people often ask, "How long would it take to deliver this particular project? How much would it cost?"

Equivocating and hesitating to give them an answer will engender distrust. Instead, use a familiar metaphor to help them understand how difficult it is to know how much something costs when it hasn't been designed.

Think about building a house. Without the blueprints, you can only guess at the house's cost.

What if you were to go to a builder and ask "how much does a house cost?"

The builder will of course say, "Well, that all depends. Is it a one-bedroom or is it a five-bedroom? Is it a mansion or is it a shack? Do you want brick or wood on the outside?"

Before a builder gives you a quote, they first need to know a lot of specific information about what materials are used, how big it is, and what kind of foundation you're going to lay underneath it. These are all important factors. People understand you must first pay someone to produce the blueprints of your home—to do the design—and you must make dozens of trade-off decisions before you know how much the house will cost to build.

When people ask "How much is it going to cost?" and I only have a fuzzy idea about the project requirements, I quickly pull out this metaphor.

Set expectations while you can deliver a ballpark estimate, but a firm cost only comes after the design is completed. After you've developed the blueprints, give them a firm cost as to what the timeline and the actual fees are going to be.

■ CHARGE EXPEDITE FEES FOR AGGRESSIVE SCHEDULES

What happens once you produce a project estimate, but are then told you need to deliver the project more quickly to get the product on the market faster?

In most cases you can shorten the timeline. Recall the Time/Quality/Cost triangle. If you change the timeline, then quality or cost must change.

In these cases I usually opt to add in an expedite fee, an additional project cost that allows me to hire contractors or dole out bonuses as incentives to have team members give me an extra burst of productivity.

■ DOCUMENT ESTIMATE THOROUGHLY

Make sure you document your estimation thoroughly. Write down your estimate and include the assumptions you made to create the estimate.

If you say something is going to cost a certain amount to deliver within a given timeline, make sure you notate the assumptions you used to create your estimate.

Even if the notes are never used or distributed to anyone but yourself, record this information. This way, if you need to go back and revise your estimate at any point, you understand how it was you came up with those numbers.

Don't take anything for granted when documenting. When you start a project, even working conditions—like having a PC, version control software or other infrastructure items—are things you can't necessarily take for granted. You want to put those in writing, particularly if you are a consultant and you have little control or history with your customer.

If you're concerned about who is going to staff your team, detail out "We assume we'll have two senior developers and three mid-tier experienced developers." Document these items and make them publicly available when feasible. If changes occur which disrupt your project delivery, you have an audit trail to point out how the environment has changed and, therefore, how the cost and timeline will need to change.

Make sure your estimates are recorded with an audit trail. Often this is as simple as sending off an e-mail to the project stakeholders so there's a record of the estimate. If features or requirements change you can remind people about your previous statements. If you don't have this documented, people will have executive amnesia—they'll perceive the change as a slip. It will be a black mark on you.

■ LEVERAGE BUDGET TEMPLATES

Maintain a budget template based on past projects. Every time you do an estimate, log it and keep it archived. Eventually (it may be nine months or three years later) having a budget template for a specific kind of project will help you. You can go back and see in past history how long it took to build a certain thing. Having prior budget templates gives you a good baseline to create future estimates.

By having project plans from prior projects you worked on (especially if you're working for a larger company where you can pool together a large volume of project plans) you can see all the tasks in other people's plans for similar projects. This helps you identify easy-to-miss critical path items.

For example, a common mistake for rolling out web systems is to forget to submit a DNS change request far enough in advance to accommodate the project's go-live date. I've seen multiple web projects waiting an additional three days beyond their target delivery date for DNS changes to propagate throughout the Internet, allowing end users to point to a new web site.

Reviewing past project plans allows you to take advantage of previous lessons learned. Budget templates give you better visibility and confidence in estimating and planning your current projects.

■ PLAN AHEAD FOR CHANGE

Change can and will occur.

Publish a change request form and make it known. I saw one vendor that did a great job of this. When they gave me their contract with their terms of service, they attached to it a change request form. They knew people were going to ask for additions to their services. By including a change request form they helped set expectations. "If you want to make changes, that's fine, but there are going to be additional fees to provide that new service."

Implement a change control board for scope changes. This can be a simple, informal thing. Stakeholders need to be invited into a meeting to approve any changes. If the situation warrants, it can also be a more formal thing where stakeholders have to sign off on release forms to approve system changes.

Whatever mechanism you use to approve changes, make sure there's a *known process* and a *known set of people* that approve feature requests. If you don't have this in place, you'll get scope creep.

When change requests come in, encourage people to roll changes into a future release. Because you have release cycles taking place in three months or less, this is a very do-able thing. Get people to wait two or three months for a particular feature, don't add it to the current development project.

Having compressed time cycle projects mitigates a lot of issues surrounding feature requests. In the old days when people were delivering six to nine month projects, scope creep was really often an understandable thing. Users didn't want to have to wait nine months to see a feature. But with these shorter projects, encourage people to defer new features until a future release.

Chapter 6 Summary

Put the Lid on Cost Overruns

- Use lethal prioritization—will it kill the project not to have that feature?

Speak the Same Language

- Define 'Happy days,' 'LOE,' and 'COB' to your team.

Use the 1.25/1.5/2.0 Rule

- Pad Straightforward Projects by 25%.
- Pad Projects with Risk Factors by 50%.
- Pad Cutting Edge Projects by 100%.

Out of the Ballpark Estimates

- Make sure initial rough estimates are out of the ballpark.

Don't Give In To Browbeating

- The first quote you give your customer—the one that really makes the client gasp—is inevitably the right one.

Be Realistic About Utilization

- Typically, team members are only available 80 percent of the time.
- Account for developer turnover and vacations.

Get Buy-in From Participants

- Have people double-check your numbers.
- Get buy-in from the people who are going to be working on the project.

No Quotes Without Blueprints

- A firm cost comes only after the design is completed.

Charge Expedite Fees for Aggressive Schedules

- If you change the timeline, then quality or cost must change.
- If you must shorten your timeline or add features, add in an expedite fee to the project cost.

Document Estimates Thoroughly

- Create an audit trail by writing down estimates.
- Include assumptions made to create the estimate.

Leverage Budget Template

- Log project plans and budgets to serve as baselines for future estimates.

Plan Ahead for Change

- Implement a change control board to deal with scope changes.
- Encourage people to roll changes into a future release.

7

Finalized Plan

How many documents do you need formalized and approved before you conclude the planning stage? The answer will vary. Don't add more 'ceremony' into your project than is necessary. But do make sure you have the core documents crafted that you need to chart your course, and provide an audit trail of what you were asked to deliver.

■ PROJECT PLAN ARTIFACTS

Business tools useful to finalize your project plans include:

- **Market Analysis**—Market gaps outlined with a full-scale positioning strategy.

- **Business Case**—Cost justification for the project initiative.

- **Product Roadmaps**—Various high-level views of planned development initiatives.

- **Objective Statement**—Business objectives for a software project.

- **Requirements Definition**—Requirements spelled out in multiple documents: candidate features list, prioritized Phase I features, and a working estimate.

- **Conceptual UI**—Multiple conceptual mockups.

- **Architecture**—A candidate architecture based on an 'off-the-shelf' proven solution.

- **Partner Selections**—Vendors including application service providers, professional services firms, and hosting providers.

- **RFP**—Request for proposal documents used to solicit proposals from vendors.

After you have identified the resources to implement your requirements, you are now ready to pull together the final pieces! But before you start to draft the project plan, take time to consider ways to rapidly deliver your system.

■ TIME TO MARKET THROUGH PARALLELISM

For decades, software project managers have labored to deliver systems quickly within budget. Why then do so many projects fail?

One answer is *speed.* By the time you deliver the system, often times a year or more after the system was initially conceived, the market has changed. Technology advances. Users change their work habits. Markets evolve as consumers adopt new buying patterns. Delivering software quickly is not an option anymore. Rapid time-to-market is essential for project success.

Traditional projects tend to implement project phases sequentially. Infrastructure and architecture may take weeks to set up. Formal design is completed before developers start any work. The system is near completion before marketing or sales are apprised of the new web services to be offered. Even when project construction takes a mere three months, it is often double that time before the system is rolled out, the help desk and sales staff trained, and marketing efforts begun in earnest.

The solution to delivering all elements of a web solution in Internet time is *parallelism*. Whenever possible, tasks must be done in parallel, not sequentially, and as early in the project as possible.

How?

First, organize early and communicate with the various departments involved in the project. Too often IT thinks strictly of their technical responsibilities. But remember, you are not delivering technology, you are delivering a *solution* to a business need. So think beyond the bounds of the technology, and wear your business hat. Think, "What must be done to deliver this solution effectively, and *in a timely manner?*"

Rapid time-to-market means marketing, sales, help desk staff and others departments involved in the total solution must be involved early. This is a challenge, since in doing this you require people to work with nascent, incomplete solutions.

Marketing must put together prototype ad layouts even before the product specification and final creative design is complete.

Coding of business logic must begin in many cases before the creative design and user interface standards are completed.

Quality Assurance personnel must write test plans even though the project specifications and features will likely change before testing begins in earnest.

Technology facilitates this new paradigm. For example, create a multimedia presentation that incorporates video of a walkthrough of the new web solution from an end user perspective, with voice annotations describing the systems features. These presentations can be hosted and streamed through the web, being ready during the deployment stage of the project. In many cases this saves several months of the total time of delivery since the sales team and help desk instantly receive product training from any computer in the world on demand.

■ ARCHITECTURE AND INFRASTRUCTURE

Probably the most overlooked opportunity for parallelism is technical infrastructure. With new projects there is often a gap of several weeks while servers are ordered, version control software and procedures implemented, and work-flow, bug tracking, and quality assurance systems put into place.

This gap can be eliminated or at least reduced by starting development *before* the architecture and infrastructure is in place. The advent of the ASP (Application Service Provider) model allows you to quickly rent solutions on a short term or long-term basis, including such services as:

- Application Servers
- Version Control Tools
- Project Management Systems
- Workflow Systems

Also, the advent of open source software and the abundance of commercial quality freeware software mean tools are readily available to allow developers to be productive within hours. These solutions can be interim solutions while the long term infrastructure is selected and implemented.

■ THE COST OF PARALLELISM

Parallelism is not without its cost. To compress the project stages into this shortened time span, you often introduce 're-do' work. For example, there is a conversion cost to using a rented server to do prototyping and then converting to a new internal server once the machine arrives.

There is a price to pay for rework. This price is small when compared to the benefit of quickly delivering software to market.

Studies have shown 60% of IT projects fail. Why so high? One reason is having solutions delivered so late to market that they are no longer relevant. How much does it cost to deliver a solution to a problem that no longer exists? A lot!

> *Include 'rework' time into your project if you use temporary infrastructure solutions or have feature or UI changes that will cause developers, marketing or other staff rework later in the project.*

■ PROJECT PLAN

Preliminary Project Plan

Put together a first cut at a project plan. This will be very rough—it may be as simple as a one page high-level overview of the project components. It is a working 'straw man' plan to help drive preliminary budgets and timelines.

Budget

Put together a budget for at least the first part of the project, with guesses as to the total cost of the project. This will be revised as the project develops.

Staffing Plan

Create a list of internal personnel and consultants needed for the project. This will often need to be spread out across a timeline to reflect the different stages at which personnel are brought into the project.

Team Organization Chart

It is essential to map out the reporting structure of the project team, especially in teams including a mix of both consultants and internal staff. It is helpful to illustrate the team relationships with a diagram showing the relationship of vendors and internal staff.

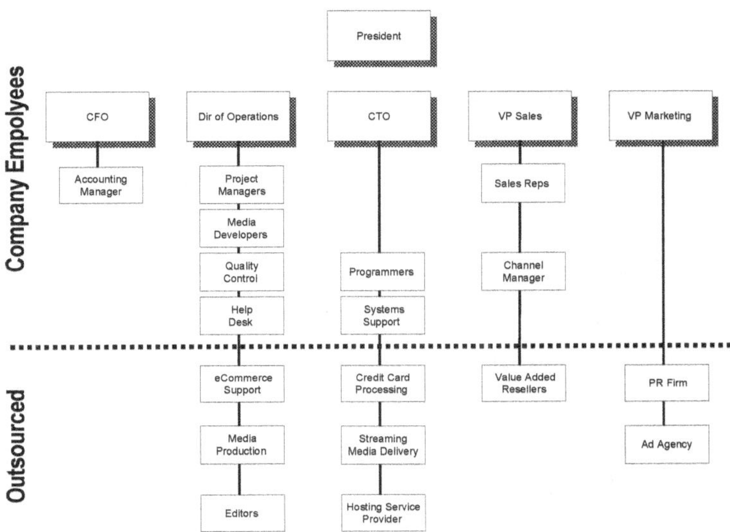

Vendors/Internal Staff Org Chart

■ PUTTING IT ALL TOGETHER

The planning stage is now complete. With deliverables such as the business case, preliminary project plan, timeline, budget and staffing plan in hand, key stakeholders have enough visibility to the project to make a decision to continue the project as is, or to revise the project requirements.

Expect changes. Project planning is definitely an iterative process. You will loop back through parts of these planning steps until you have juggled cost and requirements to meet the business objectives of your project.

Remember, the clock is ticking! Spur the decision makers forward so your work progresses!

Chapter 7 Summary

Project Plan Artifacts

Project planning artifacts may include:

- Market Analysis
- Business Case
- Product Roadmaps
- Objective Statement
- Requirements (Candidate Features List, Prioritized Phase I Features, and Working Estimate)
- Conceptual UI
- Architecture
- RFP Responses
- Partner Selections

Time to Market through Parallelism

- To speed time to market, tasks must be done in parallel, not sequentially.
- Innovative use of web-based product walkthroughs aids training support, sales, and other internal staff.

Architecture and Infrastructure

- Take advantage of hosted applications, hosted servers, and free or trial software to allow development to start in advance of architecture and infrastructure being completed.

The Cost of Parallelism

- Include 'rework' time into your project to accommodate the overhead of utilizing parallel development techniques.

Final Project Plan

The final project plan will include these artifacts:

- **Preliminary Project Plan**—a working 'straw man' plan to help drive preliminary budgets and timelines.
- **Budget**—working estimate of the total cost of the project. This will be revised as the project develops.
- **Staffing Plan**—list of internal personnel and consultants needed for the project.
- **Team Organization Chart**—reporting structure of the project team.

Step 2

Design

In business you get what you want by giving
other people what they want.

— Alice Foote MacDougall

8
Starting Design

At this point you have completed the initial planning stage of your project. With a preliminary project plan, initial budget, and staffing plan in hand you are now ready to start executing the initial parts of your project.

■ BUILD AN 'A' TEAM

Studies have shown top performing developers produce—quite literally!—an order of magnitude more work than the lowest performing developers. Can you afford to have 'cheap' talent who only produce 10% of the work of your best team members?

I quickly assess and categorize people I come in contact with as 'A' players, 'B' players and 'C' players.

'A' players are the top five percent of the talent out there. 'B' players are the next thirtieth percentile, and 'C' players are the bottom sixty-fifth percentile.

Obviously getting 'C' players is the easiest recruiting job —the world is full of them! But you cannot deliver extraordinary project results unless you populate your team with extraordinary developers on your project.

I often pay a 20-percent premium to get an 'A' player to work for me. When you look at the industry averages for compensation, this seems like a lot extra to pay for people.

Let us say you are in the military and just got orders for a small, quick, but very important mission. Fly into enemy territory and blow up an enemy fuel refinery. Who would you take?

I would grab an elite group of commandos to do the job. The last thing you want on a mission requiring such speed and precision is to go in with a platoon of recent boot-camp graduates. They'll slow you down and you won't be able to manage the mission.

Web projects are like commando raids—get the best people, go in quickly and get the job done. Recruit a few good players, even if they cost more, and quickly help your project get out the door.

A smaller team comprised of higher quality talent means there are fewer people to manage. Fewer people means greater mobility. When the fire-fight gets nasty someone reliable is there to back you up and help turn the project around.

Pay a premium to get the best talent—but insist on performance.

Tales from the Trenches

It was the beginning of a class for a Fortune 100 retailer who wanted me to train some of their internal staff on web technology.

I started out by asking a little bit about each developer's background—how much did they know about Internet development?

It wasn't terribly surprising to see almost none of them knew even the basics about web development—HTML fundamentals, Java coding basics and the like. What was shocking was discovering what they did for a living.

Most of them had been working on maintaining and developing several key Internet systems. "You've been working on developing these web projects when you haven't been given training at all on any of the technologies?", I asked incredulously.

They replied, "Yes, they hoped we could just pick it up on our own. We've done our best, but after six months of struggling, they finally decided to give us training."

Now, I am all for self-directed learning and independent study, but their lack of knowledge about the technologies had caused multiple projects to be delayed or even scuttled.

Moral of the story? Hire 'A' players who know the technology. Mentoring people in new development paradigms is a project in and of itself!

Don't be afraid to trim the deadwood early in the project. If someone's not performing, remove them from the team early in the project. Having a team with 'A' quality players as peers means a healthier team with good morale.

By having even just a few top caliber players on your team, you will soon start to benefit from the *talent magnetism effect*. As you recruit 'A' players they'll know other good people they like to work with. Leverage your top talent to help you find other elite players to add to your team. It is easier to staff having a few people in key positions early in the project!

First-rate people hire first-rate people; second-rate people hire third-rate people.

— Leo Rosten

■ TEAM BUILDING

Vendor Involvement

If you are outsourcing sections of your project, the responses to your RFP are in and your vendors are selected. The vendor's proposal will likely contain a firm estimate of the cost to conduct the design phase, along with a preliminary estimate to develop and deploy the project. The full project scope will be further refined during the design phase, so it is imperative the vendor who will develop the software be involved at this point. After the design phase is over you will be able to get a firm estimate on the cost of the rest of the project.

Now you can work with the vendor to firm up project details such as identifying specific personnel who will participate in the project and revising the cost estimate for the project along with its start and end dates.

Staff Ramp Up

This is an exciting time! Your core project team is now assembled. The dynamic of a new project with fresh requirements and new technologies provides a level of excitement. Capitalize on this.

There may be people working together for the first time and getting to know one another. Other personnel may have prior project experience with other co-workers on the team. You may also have consultants on board who will play a role on your project team.

When outside vendors are teamed with in-house staff, it is your responsibility to make the outsiders feel part of the team, while at the same time keeping your internal resources non-threatened by the influx of external personnel.

The staff dynamic that contributes to project success or failure will be established early. It is imperative to identify any personality conflicts and other personnel problems early on. Removing a problem team member half way through the project is demoralizing and costly. Do not be afraid to pull the trigger and deal with problems early in the project. Your team will respect you if you deal decisively with such issues!

The beginning of a project is a time of high-energy and excitement. Help your team realize the importance of your objectives. People will put their heart into a project once they understand change is really going to happen, and the project they are working on is going to make a difference.

Make consultants feel at home. Do not draw sharp lines of distinctions between internal staff and outside consultants. Creating an 'us versus them' mentality will dampen productivity. At the same time, take care not to alienate your staff by allowing arrogant consultants to make your staff feel inferior. Have private conversations with all your team members early in the project to identify any issues.

Take proactive actions to build team moral and stifle negativity. Above all, build esprit de corps by being positive, energetic and excited. Enthusiasm is contagious!

■ DESIGN OVERVIEW

The first part of the design phase consists of a series of design meetings with key members of your project team. These sessions are discussions with end users to flesh out the system design. Depending on the project, end users may be internal employees, customers or some combination of the two.

Create an online environment where the end users can communicate with one another and provide feedback. This may take the form of a password protected web site, newsgroups, message boards and private chat rooms. Following the initial project release, this area can continue to be a source of feedback from the end user community.

Begin each meeting by discussing the current candidate features list. The design meetings define how the requirements logically relate to each other to form a system design.

Initial Design

In the initial design meetings you identify roles and scenarios within the system. Initial design is complete once you have a 'straw man' prototype of the user interface completed, ready for review by the end users. You also create a glossary and supplemental specifications as an ongoing part of the design process.

This design phase is focused on the *end user*—getting them to describe how they wish to interact with the system. Your project team should concentrate on guiding discussion to flesh out all the roles and scenarios. Listen a lot; create diagrams, flow charts and UI sketches, and take copious notes.

Detailed Design

Detailed design is very *developer* intensive. Your team takes the information gleaned from the initial end user design meetings and puts flesh on the bones of your skeleton design.

Developers create a site map and a series of visual use cases to identify any additional business rules or technical requirements of the system. Review these with the end users for accuracy.

Significant behind the scenes work is done to design the systems technology by creating a data model and, when applicable, an object model. Additional considerations such as scaling requirements are also evaluated.

Acceptance

Acceptance is the final design phase in which you annotate the Site Map with Use Cases, create an Online Storyboard and update the Visual Use Cases. After updating the project plan and revising the budget and timeline, get final approval to move on to the development phase.

■ GETTING STARTED

Project Kickoff Meeting

Hold a project kickoff meeting. Invite your current project team members, plus any other key stakeholders such as the project sponsor and representative members from the user community who will benefit from this project.

During the kickoff meeting, review the objective statement for the project. This is an excellent opportunity to focus attention on the goals of the project.

Take care to manage expectations. Now that you have buy-in from stakeholders on the requirements of the project, do not entertain new software features! Do not allow scope creep to lengthen the cost and timeline.

Make sure to cover these points in the meeting:

- Metrics used to measure project success or failure.
- Key stakeholders needed to make the business decisions necessary to move the project forward.
- Team member reporting structure—who reports to whom.
- Team members and their roles.
- Division of responsibilities between internal staff and outside vendors.
- Periodic reporting structures are needed.
- Recap of the objective statement.

Manage Expectations

Effectively managing expectations is the surest way to project success! Review the objective statement up front, communicate and deal with issues as they arise, and be honest and forthright about project realities.

Bad news delayed only makes bad news worse. Inflated expectations about the functionality or benefits of a system will make the project seem a failure even if it is successful from a technical perspective.

Validate Architecture

You should validate your system architecture. If any key technologies to be used in the project are new to your team, test them to identify technical problems early on. Do not simply believe a vendor's marketing pitch about how great a technology is. See if it works for you!

One way to do this is called a 'thin slice approach.' With this technique you create a prototype system that implements—at a very simple level—each and every component of your system. For example, have your e-commerce storefront talk successfully to your backend merchants, and your application server talk to any integrated backend systems and your database.

Use a 'Thin Slice' approach to validate your system architecture.

Validate not only your technology selections but also your vendor selections. Take time to call your vendor's support lines and check out their responsiveness. Have your 'thin slice' system working early on to exercise the vendor's software. If you identify any integration or support difficulties early on, you have the luxury of fixing the problems or even selecting another vendor before you continue further development.

■ KEEP IT SIMPLE

Part of the art of delivering systems in Internet time is to find the sweet spot of project management. Most formal software development methodologies were created during the era of mammoth, monolithic software projects spanning multiple months—sometimes even years! The management controls of legacy systems are elaborate and often bureaucratic. They may make sense for a one-year project but are overkill for shorter, nimble projects.

The compressed business cycles of recent years demand a significantly shortened project life cycle. In this new break-neck speed world, formal management methods just don't work.

Unfortunately, web developers and web project managers are usually working too fast to take time from their project pressures to discover a lightweight approach to successfully manage their projects.

> *All other things being equal, the simplest solution is usually the correct one.*
>
> *— William of Occam*

Simplicity is the fastest and least expensive way to accomplish work. Simplicity fosters re-usability and security. Keeping your methodology simple and your code small and clean will help you manage and control your project to a successful conclusion. Web project managers need a methodology that gives them control of and visibility to their project. Developing with web speed demands a new methodology with small delivery cycles, and simplified management constructs.

Right Sized Design

You need to design—but only to a certain point.

The final design of software is always done in the trenches by the developers themselves. I have seen elaborate object models with hundreds of classes constructed with great care, only to see the final product look nothing like the original design phase model.

> ***80% of design is done in the trenches.***

Micro-Releases

The rule of thumb is to get the project done in three months, no matter what. If the project is bigger than something that can be delivered in three months, then break up the project into smaller pieces.

Do all projects need to take 3 months? Not necessarily. I have coined a phrase called 'micro-releases'—short 2 or 3 week projects that add a few simple features. You code, test and quickly deliver the feature to the end users. Features which didn't make the first 3 month cycle can be delivered later, 'just-in-time,' using micro-releases.

In most cases, your initial release just needs to be 'barely usable'—a minimalist, small features system—to be in production. This core initial release should contain only the 'must have' features to make the system viable. Defer all other feature requests until later phases.

No matter what users say, they do not really know what they want until they start using the software!

You must show clients something they can react to. Only once it is in their hands do you really start to get good feedback on the features they really need.

> **End users cannot tell you what they want until they see it .**

■ MAKE 80% DECISIONS

Project planning is not an exact science. Projects stall and timelines grow as team leaders collect enough information and ponder over the right decision.

When you start a project, you don't have perfect information. This is nothing to be alarmed at of course. The dutiful project manager ensures time and cost estimates are sufficiently padded to account for *not* having perfect information.

There is an 80/20 axiom that has been successfully applied to all kinds of business generalities. It applies perfectly to decision theory. It takes 20% of your time and effort to produce 80% of the information you need to make a decision. Beyond this, it would take 80% of your time to come up with the remaining 20% of the information that would factor into your business decision.

You have to settle for 80 percent accuracy. This will give you the biggest bang for the buck. You're not really going to know 100 percent of all the information you need to make perfect decisions until the end of the project.

Because we have short project life cycles of three months or less, making a decision based on 80% of the facts is perfectly acceptable. The risk of not having perfect information is greatly mitigated because you have such a short life cycle.

The minimized scope of the project you're undertaking with its pared down feature set reduces the variables that cause project management to spiral into management complexity. With a much shorter calendar timeframe to deal with, your decision-making cycle is compressed and much more manageable.

Having a good plan now is better than having a perfect plan months from now. So do your best, use the 80/20 rule to make decisions and get your project quickly underway and on the path to completion!

■ INITIAL DESIGN

Roles

During your design meetings you identify roles. Different sets of users have different roles within the system. Hardware and software APIs also have roles in some cases.

Users

Who are the users of this system? Common user roles include customers, customer service representative, system administrator, accounts receivable and technical support.

If the users exhibit different system usage it is often helpful to segment these roles further. For example, customers might be divided into technophobes and technophiles. The technophobe customer may refuse to give their credit card out on a web site, and so the system flow will need to accommodate telephone and fax credit card orders. The technophile customers follow the normal system flow of entering the credit card online.

You should compile a list with the name of each user group. Accompany each group with a paragraph defining their role.

Security Roles

Most advanced systems have security requirements. As you identify user roles, start to ask questions about what security privileges each group of users should have. Jot down these security requirements alongside the user's role description.

System Roles

People are not the only actors within your system to have roles. We also define *systems* as having roles. Systems in this definition includes hardware servers, vendor services, e-commerce APIs—even client-side end user software.

The key to defining system roles is to first define the system boundary. The system boundary is the border that defines the system you are creating. For example, an e-commerce web site might contain shopping cart software which runs in conjunction with a web server and a database server. It talks in real time to an outside credit card processing vendor. In this example, a diagram illustrating the system shows the system boundary as a box around your internal software and servers. The credit card processing vendor functions as a role and is pictured as an outside actor interacting with your core system.

Like user roles, system roles have security requirements. A piece of e-commerce software that is installed and runs on your server should be given restricted access on your server.

Scenarios

Scenarios start as simple sentences describing a particular set of user interactions with the system.

Examples of Scenarios

✔ New user registers for the first time.

✔ Existing user orders a product.

✔ Administrator maintains catalog information.

✔ System downloads batch reports from e-commerce vendor.

Initially you want to brainstorm with your design team and come up with as many basic scenarios as you can. Then logically group them and distill them into a list of scenarios to form the core of your system.

This scenarios list will serve as a guide for constructing the user interface. Later on these will become the use cases for the system.

Page Flow Tree View

With the scenario list in hand, create a simple text-based tree view outline of pages to be accessed within each scenario. One powerful way to collaborate in page flow design is to assemble your technical team in a room with a projector hooked up to a computer. Using a simple word processor you can quickly throw together a candidate page flow.

Why start with text? Because it is easy and quick to work with. You can rough up your site map in text format. After you have the page flow fairly established, start formally diagramming the site map.

Here is an example of a page flow tree view of a scenario:

```
            Member Login/Registration Scenario

Credit Card Purchase

→ Credit Card

        → Verify Purchase

                → Purchase Results/Receipt

Coupon Purchase

→ Coupon

        → Verify Purchase

                → Purchase Results/Receipt
```

Create the text-based tree view page flow for each scenario. As you walk through the page flows with your team you can quickly add in missing pages and modify the page flow.

After completing a tree view page flow for your system, create a site map. The site map should be created in a diagramming tool. It is essentially a flow chart showing the navigation of the system. This will help your team understand the flow of the system, and will facilitate communication with end users to help validate the system requirements.

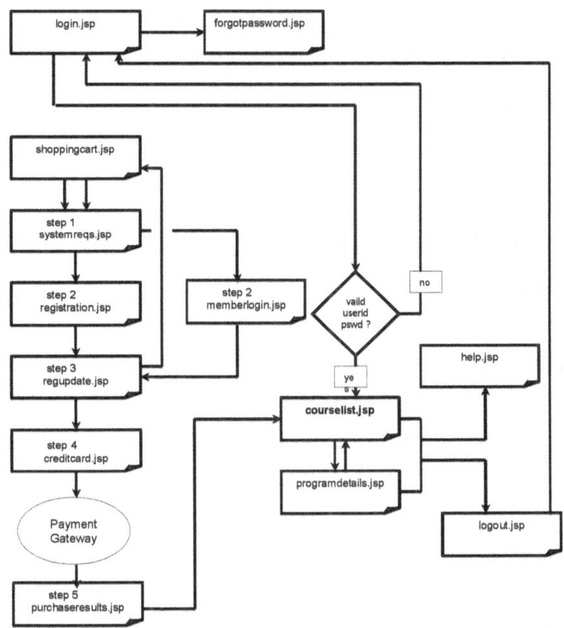

Site Map

Project Glossary

Assemble a project glossary in the initial design meetings. Language is important. Almost all markets, companies, and industries have special terms they use. The project glossary is a short dictionary quickly defining the distinctive language used by the design team.

The project glossary is a living document defined early but revised throughout the life of the project. Team members joining the project after the initial design is done will find this list a valuable tool to quickly learn the language needed to master understanding of the system.

Common examples of generic terms that may need definition for your project:

'Customer'

Is this someone who visits your web site as a prospect? Or is it only defined as those who have purchased a product from you?

If you resell your services, then your customers (the ones who private label or sell your services) will have their own set of customers. In this case you need terms to distinguish your direct customer versus the reseller's clients.

'Member'

Some groups such as associations have complex notions of what defines a member. Your web site will have visitors who are prospective members. They may even purchase products or perform other member-like functions. These prospects may even register for secure access to areas of you site, yet still they are not an official member since they have not paid membership dues. You may choose to use terms like candidate, prospect, participant and member to define these various roles.

One final note: while it is important to document a project glossary, it is also important to minimize the number of technical acronyms and buzzwords you use. Speak in the language of your end user.

Supplementary Specifications

The supplementary specifications list is a compilation of 'other' project requirements. These are requirements not quite fitting into any other category.

Like the project glossary, the supplementary specifications document is started early in the project, but can be annotated at any stage of the project life cycle.

Most of the supplementary specifications are defined early in the project. Since these are system requirements, any additions will impact system scope, budget and timeline.

Example Supplementary Specifications

✔ End users must have the latest version of Microsoft Internet Explorer™ and Macromedia Flash™ to run the system.

✔ International access to the system requires a content distribution network allowing high speed access to the system in both North America, Europe, and Southeast Asia.

✔ ADA (Americans with Disabilities Act) compliance requires the user interface to have special HTML tags which can be read by sight-impaired audio HTML readers.

Chapter 8 Summary

Build an 'A' Team

- Pay a premium to get the best talent—but insist on performance.

Team Building

- Involve any vendors and consultants with your staff early on as you assemble your team.

Getting Started

- Hold a project kickoff meeting.

- Manage expectations to ensure project success.

- Validate architecture using a thin-slice approach.

Keep It Simple

- Break big projects down into small three-month-or-less micro-releases.

- Use a lightweight project management method to gain appropriate control and visibility to the project.

Use the 80/20 Rule to Make Decisions

- An imperfect decision now is better than a perfect decision three months from now!

Initial Design

- Define user roles, security roles and system roles.

- Create scenarios list.

- Use page flow tree views to quickly layout the system flow.

- Create the site map as a visual flow chart of the system.

- Maintain project glossary and supplementary specifications lists throughout the life of the project.

9
Detailed Design

With the requirements defined and the page flow of the system laid out, your development team is ready to start detailed design. Technical members of your team will break off into sub-teams to work on visual use cases, an object model, a database schema and other pre-implementation design deliverables.

■ VISUAL USE CASES

The scenarios defined so far have only a simple text description. Now create a visual use case for each scenario.

Entire books have been written on the topic of software design using use cases. I like to use a visually annotated version of use case modeling that is optimized for web design.

Whereas most design documents such as page flow diagrams and database models depict *design time* information, the visual use case is focused on representing *run time* information about the system. It shows how the system behaves from an end user perspective for any given scenario.

Each visual use case is given a name, usually the name of the scenario defined earlier.

The use case is then broken down into four major parts:

Part 1: Description

Actors

Actors are roles which participate in the visual use case. Examples include user roles like customers or administrators, or system roles like third party e-commerce systems interfacing with your software.

Purpose

The purpose describes why the system is engaged in this particular scenario.

Brief Description

This is a summarized description of the actions taking place within the visual use case.

Pre-conditions

This identifies what pre-conditions were met in order for this scenario to occur. For example, a user is required to have an Internet connection, a browser running and have logged in prior to the scenario occurring.

Part 2: Flow

The flow lays out in table format the actor actions and the system responses.

Typical flow

The typical flow is what normally occurs within the system.

Exception flows

Exception flows are for atypical user situations and system error conditions. For example:

Example Exception Flows

✔ The user's Zip code does not pass validation rules.

✔ The user's credit card charge is declined and cannot be processed.

✔ The user clicks the back button while a credit card payment is being processed.

✔ The credit card payment vendor is offline.

✔ The end user's Internet connection drops during a transaction.

✔ The user does not have a browser capable of the 128-bit encryption required.

Part 3: Comments

These are miscellaneous comments on the visual use case.

Business Rules

This is a list of any relevant business rules in action for this use case. Some examples:

Example Business Rules

✔ Only accept American dollars for payment.

✔ Do not assess shipping and handling charges for the first phase of the project.

✔ Only accept online orders; do not offer checks in the mail, phone credit card orders or other forms of payment.

Post Conditions

Post conditions describe the state of the scenario after the visual use case has been completed.

Issues

This is a catch-all section used to describe any issues relating to the visual use case. It is a project management tool used during the design phase to help resolve design issues. Ideally you should not start development on a project until all design issues regarding a visual use case have been resolved. During design, a section under the visual use cases's issues section can be added to indicate if the end users or project stakeholders have approved the visual use case or not.

Assumptions

This section includes assumptions and forward thinking statements such as:

Example Assumptions

✔ Do credit card charges through Acme Payment Services.

✔ Use Acme's PayrightPro API to process credit card transactions.

✔ Phase II of the project will possibly expand payment support to include telephone and fax credit card orders.

Part 4: User Interface

Screen Shots

This section may be blank for the moment. Later it will include mocked-up screen-shots of the user interface taken from the storyboard created during final design. You can also make preliminary notes here on additional UI requirements such as menu navigation or JavaScript actions.

Page Flow

This is the tree view page flow outline identified during initial design.

Use Case: Ordering a Product

Description

Actors
End user

Purpose
To log into the member portal to verify access privileges before accessing training and testing services.

Brief Description
The end user logs in order to access the services they have paid for.

Pre-conditions
End user has an Internet connection and a browser running. This use case may be entered once the actor has successfully logged in to the system.

Flow

Typical Flow

Actor Actions	System Response
1. This use case begins when the user selects to enter a new order.	2. Asks the user for the customer phone number.
3. The user enters the customer phone number.	4. Presents the customer information and a new order form to the user.
5. The user adds products onto the order form.	6. Updates the price quote on the order form.
7. The user indicates that the order is complete.	8. Asks the user to verify customer credit information.
9. The user verifies the information.	10. Checks the credit and displays a message indicating "credit approved." (The system will also update the inventory information). Exception Flow #1: System determines that the credit card number is not correct. Exception Flow #2: Authorization service declines transaction

Exception Flow #1: "Credit card information not correct"

Actor Actions	System Response
9. The user determines that a different credit card is to be used. The user enters the new credit card information. The basic course continues.	

Exception Flow #2: "Credit not approved"

Actor Actions	System Response
	10. Checks the credit. The credit is not approved. The system alerts the user that the credit has not been approved.
11. The user enters new credit information. The basic course resumes.	

(download a soft copy template from stanshinn.com)

Sample Use Case (Page 1)

Use Case: Ordering a Product

Comments

Business Rules
None

Post Conditions
A phone order has been successfully processed.

Issues
Need to get end-user to sign off on use case

Comments
None

User Interface

Screenshots

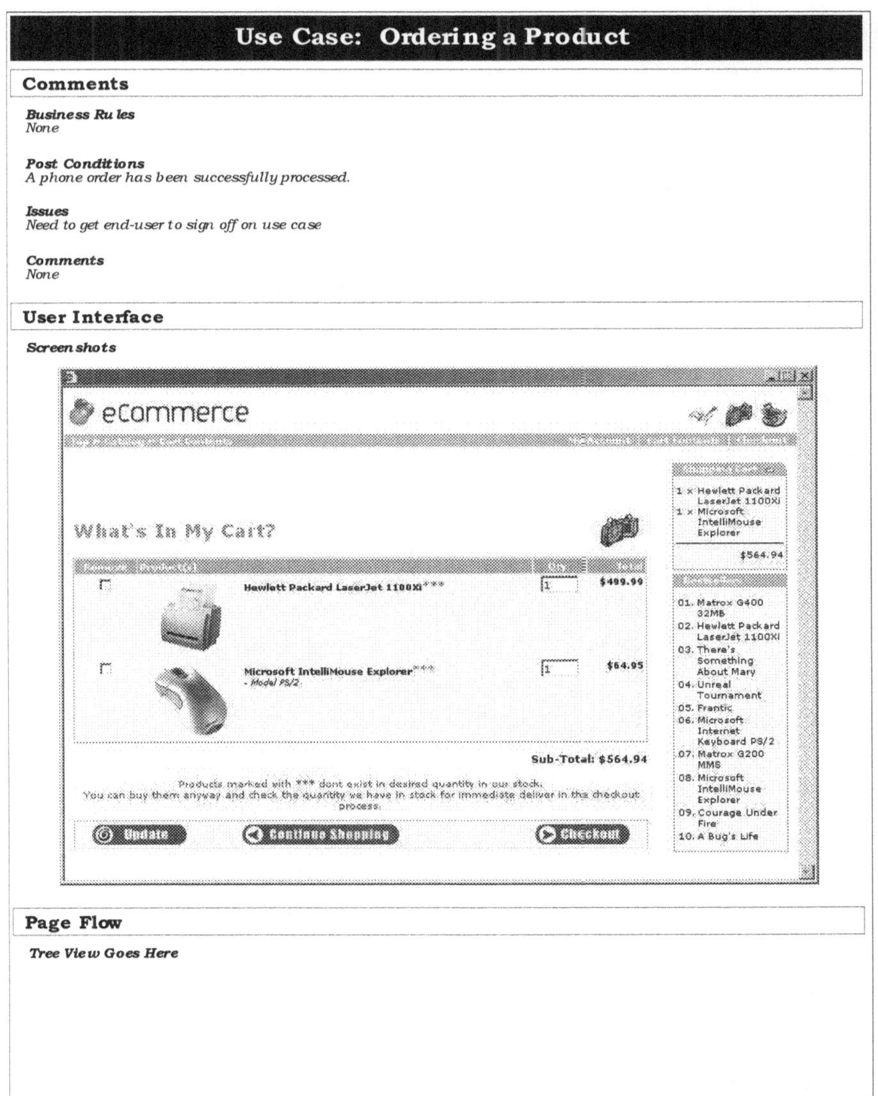

Page Flow

Tree View Goes Here

Sample Use Case (Page 2)

■ SCALING

Assess the scaling requirements of the system. What hardware, software and network capacity are needed to meet these requirements?

Scalability is one of the trickiest aspects of web project design. In many ways it is more of an art than a science. If your team does not have prior experience in delivering system capacity to scale to the required level, it is wise to pay consultants to validate that your system design will scale appropriately.

Flash Crowds

The Internet user base is not at all like Client/Server or legacy systems' user bases. Historically, users have been internal employees who accessed the system primarily during business hours. Their system usage was fairly constant.

Web systems often experience periodic surges in users called 'flash crowds'. Spikes to your system can be exponentially many times greater than normal usage. Consumer oriented systems are such that seasonal spikes during pay days, end of the month, holidays and other special occasions can overwhelm your system if you are unprepared. If a consumer hits a slow site or one that cannot process their order, they are just a few clicks away from taking their business to your competitor.

Scaling Metrics

How do you plan for such spike usage? The answer varies. Once the system is in place for a while, statistics on system usage patterns will be available. However, you will not have this information up front.

Consumer oriented systems follow these general metrics:

- The busy day of the month is 5% of your total monthly traffic.
- The busy hour of the day is 8% of your total daily traffic.
- The busy hour of the month is 0.4% of your total traffic.
- Most users sit idle for 95% of their session. 95% of the time they are reading HTML content, filling out a web form or simply thinking. Only 5% of the time are they clicking on a link or submitting a form.
- Other metrics that you will need to determine, based on the specifications of your particular system:

  1) Average page load time.

  2) Average time the typical user is on the system (their session length).

  3) Number of pages accessed within a typical user session. (It may be helpful for you to define this by scenario.)

After the system is live and there is actual history of system usage, you can refine your scaling metrics. With these in hand you can plan and implement a system to effectively respond to your production needs.

Scalable Networks

If you anticipate flash crowds and you have a consumer user base, you should investigate using a commercial content delivery network. Content delivery networks (CDNs) specialize in providing network architectures optimized to handle flash crowd capacity. CDNs use 'edge servers' with proprietary routing mechanisms and real-time Internet monitoring conditions. CDNs serve your content faster and more reliably than standard network providers.

■ DATA DESIGN

Database design is the core of your backend system. Initial database design begins after requirements are fleshed out in visual use case design.

At this point we refer to the database schema under development as the candidate data model. Although you should try to establish the design in as much detail as possible, much of the database design will not be done until you are in the midst of development.

Database changes taking place after the development stage begins are expensive. Changing the schema after code development has begun may require rework. Many web project leaders include rework into their project plans as a matter of course.

Having a good database administrator is integral to success. If you do not have a database administrator knowledgeable about optimizing the database for speed, hire a consultant to advise you in this process.

> *If your system needs to be scalable, the number one area to optimize for fast system performance is the database.*

Use a professional data modeling tool to layout your database schema. Make the latest copy of the data model readily available to developers through your project intranet.

■ OBJECT DESIGN

Advanced enterprise systems may use reusable software objects. The object modeling process closely follows the database design process.

Make sure team members have access to the object model so they understand the classes and objects that are available to them during development.

Tales from the Trenches

The excitement was palpable as our project team used a CRC (Class-Responsibility-Collaborator) Card design session to flesh out an object model. The system was going to be extremely modular and object-oriented, utilizing the latest object design tool to lay out the classes within our web system.

Three months later we looked back on our initial design. Our system had been knocked out in record time, ahead of schedule and under budget. But had we faithfully followed our object design when we wrote our system? Not at all!

In the trenches, we discovered numerous new implementation details had radically altered our classes and their methods. We had an object-oriented system, but it used far fewer classes than we had mapped out. The complex design had yielded to the far simpler and more practical code done in the trenches of development.

Do I still recommend object models and object design techniques? Only on the most complex systems. For most business systems, web design should be focused on scripting and calling modular, reusable func-

---

> *tions or web services. Today I leave complex, well documented object oriented design to the creators of word processors, rocket guidance systems and complex commercial software packages. For everyday use, I toss the object models in favor of code that works, and is developed fast.*

If the system is complex, use an object modeling tool to layout the object design. In larger shops it is also beneficial to have an Object Administrator who manages the object model and facilitates code reuse. Periodic code reviews help encourage developers to make appropriate use of the object model.

If your team is big enough, consider dividing the group into backend business object developers and front-end UI developers. Both teams have to know and understand the system. Business object developers focus on SQL and reusable objects. UI developers focus on creative design and usability issues, scripting their pages to access the business logic coded by the backend developers.

> **Divide larger project teams into business object and UI development groups.**

Do not confuse reusable code and object oriented programming. Studies have shown legacy COBOL copy books have better success for re-using code than custom-built object libraries. What is important is not that you do object modeling, but rather that you make re-usable software with a simple, standardized interface that is well known to your development team.

Chapter 9 Summary

Visual Use Cases

- Visual use cases are created for each scenario, each including:

    1. **Description**—Includes Actors, Purpose, Brief Description and Pre-conditions.

    2. **Flow**—Typical flow and Exception flows, which are actor actions and the system responses in table format.

    3. **Comments**—Business Rules, Post Conditions, Issues and Assumptions.

    4. **User Interface**—Includes Screen Shots and Page Flow.

Scaling

- Define the hardware, software and network architecture needed for scalability.

- **Flash Crowds**—Plan for spike usage of your system.

- **Scaling Metrics**—Define and document the metrics you use to forecast the scalability of your system.

- **Scalable Networks**—Use CDNs as appropriate to quickly deliver content.

Data Design

- Create a conceptual data model outlining the database design for your system.

Object Design

- For large systems, create a conceptual object model.

10
Final Review

The design phase is now drawing to a close. The results should be in from any 'thin-slice' architecture evaluations you have done. Hardware and software should be purchased and installed. You may be building out infrastructure to facilitate the project development about to begin. Staff should be trained and familiar with the infrastructure before moving into development, particularly if any new technologies are being used,

After finishing touches to the system design, finalize requirements and update the project plan and budget.

■ SITE MAP WITH USE CASES

Now that the system scenarios have been refined by creating visual use cases, update your site map by noting which pages within the system correspond to the visual use cases. If there are pages within the system that do not have a corresponding scenario and visual use case, create them now. The 'Site Map with Use Cases' document is a great way to validate that no functionality has been overlooked.

You may use a diagramming tool to create the site map. You may also want to color code the site map to make it easier to view and interpret.

■ ONLINE STORYBOARD

Create static HTML pages corresponding to each page within your system. These are leveraged later on when developers start putting code behind these pages.

Make this online storyboard easy to navigate. Place comments next to buttons or links not yet functional, letting end users know it is still only a prototype.

Hold a UI review meeting with the end users to review the storyboard. Review the semi-functional UI within a browser using a computer and a projector.

Solicit comments from your end users on functionality, and take notes on your site map to document any 'tweaks' that need to be done to the user interface or page flow.

■ ANNOTATE VISUAL USE CASES

Now that you have screen shots, go back and insert the screen images into the 'screen shots' section of appropriate visual use cases.

Make notes underneath the screens within the visual use cases that describe any dynamic page elements such as button rollover effects, JavaScript actions or other page functions not previously described.

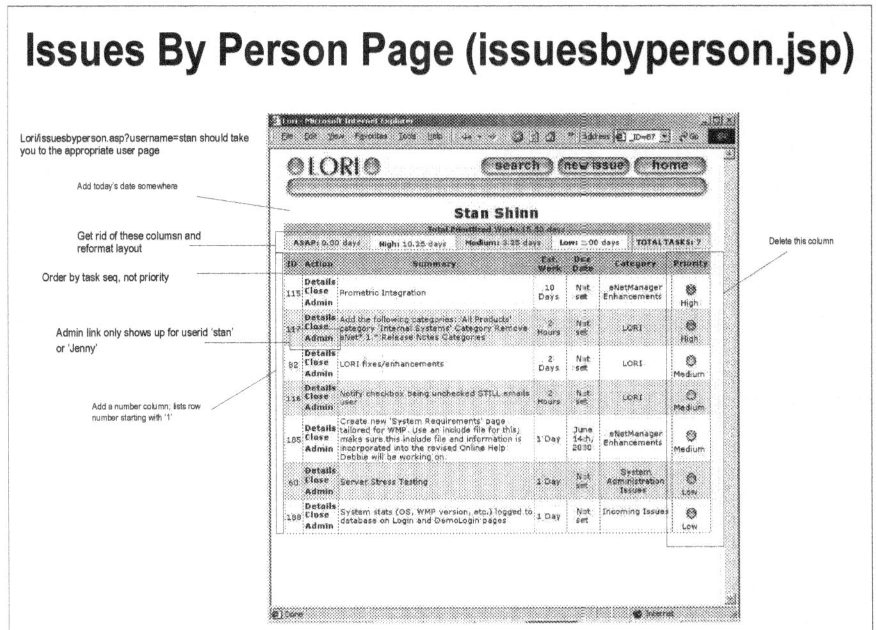

Visual Use Case

■ ACCEPTANCE

With the updated visual use cases, the site map with use cases, and an online storyboard, get final approval to move on to the development phase.

Now that design is completed, it is time to revisit the project plan. The timeline and project plan can be refined now that hardware, software, and vendor costs are known.

Get signoff from project stakeholders. In big organizations or in situations where a consulting firm is implementing a portion of the project, this often means getting a literal signature approving the design and budget. For smaller projects, an email or other informal, documented approval will often suffice.

The design phase is officially over when you have the following:

- All necessary design deliverables completed.
- A revised cost estimate for building and deploying the system.
- Project plan detailed by task down to the nearest day.
- Approval on the design from project stakeholders.

Once you are finished, compile *all* the deliverables from the design phase. Archive them in a known, shared location. Now execute your project against these baselined design requirements.

Chapter 10 Summary

Site Map With Use Cases

- Use a diagramming tool to create the color coded site map with use cases.

Online Storyboard

- Create static HTML pages corresponding to each page within your system. Hold a UI review meeting with the end users to review the storyboard. Review the semi-functional UI within a browser using a computer and a projector.

Annotate Visual Use Cases

- Insert screen images into the 'screen shots' section of appropriate visual use cases.

Modify The Project Plan

- Update the project plan. Compile all the deliverables from the design phase and archive them in a known, shared location.

Acceptance

- Get final approval to move on to the development phase.

Step 3

Develop

The only place success comes before work is in
the dictionary.

— Vince Lombardi

11
Standards

Standards such as naming conventions and those governing user interfaces are absolutely essential when developing software. Use software tools to help support the use of standards in development.

■ BENEFITS OF STANDARDS

Have coding and UI standards in place *before* beginning to code. Having standards in place early in the project promotes consistency. Consistent code will be much easier to maintain and update later in the development life cycle.

When there is a large project team and several different people touch the same section of code, having a common style and logic to how code and user interface elements are structured will make it much easier for developers to do their work.

Developers see what the prior developers were thinking when they wrote the code because there's a certain consistency to how the comments are made and a uniform structure to how the software is laid out. When tasked with enhancing code you want to concentrate on how to solve problems—you don't want to spend time decrypting an arcane, confusing piece of code! Coding standards provide the road signs to help navigate through the jungle of hundreds of thousands of lines of code.

■ CODING STANDARDS

How should comments be made in code? There are multiple ways to add notes to software. Have a style guide about how, when, and where to make comments in the code. Define the variable name conventions which will be used as well as function names, standard tools, and libraries to be included in software construction.

Another helpful thing is to have standard notation indicating a particular piece of code is 'in progress.' Often developers will be writing code and they'll need to flag it as 'in progress'—it is a piece of code under construction that someone will need to go back later and finish. It may be a temporary block of code that will need additional attention.

Even when it's your own piece of code, you may forget where those pieces are that need to be looked at again. Having some sort of notation identifying code that needs further attention is an extremely helpful thing.

Where Files are Located

Standardize where files are located. When code is checked out from the version control tool, does the code sit on the workstation or does it sit in a user directory on a file server? If on the workstation— is there a standardized directory location on the hard drive where one should put code? If a developer is on vacation and someone needs to take a look at code not checked back in, people need to know instantly where to go to find it.

■ UI STANDARDS

Another standards document helpful to have is a user interface set of standards. These guidelines will define the common look and feel, color scheme and CSS standards. Include standardized elements like the corporate logo, how big the logo is, which fonts to use, and the color palette.

All of these things need to be clearly spelled out. If this is defined early in the project it will save a lot of heartache later on.

It's a little bit like building a house. The difference between using a 2x4 and a 2x6 piece of wood is really not a huge cost difference as long as you make this decision early on in the construction of the house. But once the house is built, to then say 'Oh I want all my 2x4s to be 2x6s now' is a pretty major change. Make these decisions up front and build the firm foundation you need; don't defer these decisions until later.

The best standards documents are less than 25 pages long. Nothing too complex—just the basic fundamental issues of which people need be aware. Make it accessible so everyone understands where the conventions are located.

■ CODE REVIEWS

If your team adheres to standards and naming conventions, it won't matter who maintains the code because there is familiarity with how the software is written. Enforce these standards through code reviews. Do code reviews at milestones throughout the project.

The code reviews can take two forms. A formal code review involves the development team and the project manager. At the meeting the team walks through the code and examines the code and flow of logic within the software. This also serves as an informal knowledge transfer.

This can be quite laborious. It is really not practical to do reviews of *all* your code. Rather, work with representative sections of code, early in the project, in order to weed out bad practices and logic flaws. This gives you visibility to team members who may not be that skilled or adept at writing good code. You can focus on mentoring these individuals. As you get to know your team, you can reduce the number of code reviews as you gain confidence in the competency of your team's skills.

Pair Programming

What about the much touted notion of 'pair programming?' Pair programming is a technique some agile methodologies employ in which developers work in pairs. Each developer pair works together (usually in the same workspace!) and every piece of code has two sets of eyes looking at it.

You definitely will solve problems much more quickly with pair programming. But what about the tradeoffs? People value their privacy, and working together as Siamese twins does not make for long term happy employees. My experience has been that periodically switching developers to work on different projects or different subsystems within the same project will produce much of the needed cross-training and quality assurance that pair programming does, while preserving the dignity of the developer.

Code Swaps

Another good practice is to swap which parts of the system that a developer is writing. This practice serves as a built-in quality assurance mechanism early in the development of a project. Simply pause at a project milestone (when developers are at a logical stopping point) and re-assign the sections of the software to different developers. In doing this, you'll provide informal opportunities for peers to review code.

> ***Structure the project so that developers can have opportunities to work on multiple parts of the system.***

As developers take over these new areas of code, they are forced to understand how that sub-system works and why the code is written the way it is. If they want to know how things work or why certain coding decisions were made, they'll ask the other team members.

It's not foolproof, but it's a lot more practical than continuous group code reviews because you don't have much time to sit around and scrutinize code.

Code reviews serve not only for knowledge transfer, but also to assure the quality of the code is such that it is easily maintainable by anyone. It heads off flawed software structures and forces developers to be more accountable for their software design. Don't wait for beta testers to discover flawed software—catch it early on by introducing the peer pressure of code reviews and code swaps!

Chapter 11 Summary

Benefits of Standards

- Create standards *before* starting the project. This creates a uniform structure to how the software is laid out, making maintenance easier.

Coding Standards

- Have a style guide about how, when and where to make comments in the code.

- Specify a standard to indicate a particular piece of code is 'in progress'.

- Standardize where development files are located.

UI Standards

- Define the common look and feel, color scheme and CSS standards the team will use.

Code Reviews

- Enforce standards through code reviews.

- Pair programming is an option with tradeoffs; working together as Siamese twins does not make for long term job satisfaction.

- Implement 'code swaps' to allow peers to review code.

12

Infrastructure

It's important to have version control and configuration management tools in place early on. Putting infrastructure in place before getting deep into the heat of a project will save time, money, and heartache.

■ BUILD THE BEST ENVIRONMENT

Highly effective project managers make sure developers have the environment conducive to giving them the productivity they need.

Don't scrimp on hardware

Make sure your team has computers with fast processors and lots of memory. A few hundred dollars spent on computer hardware is a lot cheaper than squandering hundreds of hours of lost developer productivity over the course of a year!

Give them quiet and privacy

Make sure your team has a quiet environment. Just think about when you go the library. You do not make noise in the library because people are concentrating—

they're trying to read. Software development is similar. It requires an intense level of concentration, much like a mathematician or a surgeon.

Many have experimented with things like open work bays and low-walled cubes to "encourage communications." These are *not* effective. In the end, it fosters resentment and hurts productivity because people actually like and need privacy.

Software development is a thinking intensive art requiring concentration. Studies have shown, within a quiet private environment you are much more productive than working in an open work bay or an open cubicle. Make sure you provide thinking-conducive work environments.

Avoid 'Thrashing'

Another thing you can do to ensure your developers have the best, most productive environment possible is to help your developers avoid what I call 'thrashing.' Thrashing is when developers are constantly interrupted with new information or additional tasks.

Carve out long periods of time for your developers to concentrate on the work they're doing. Divide work so your team has three and four hour blocks of time to work in peace and quiet. When developers get called on the phone every 30 minutes or have impromptu meetings, it's hard for them to focus and be productive.

Tales from the Trenches

There I was, lecturing to a room of eager web developers, witnessing what must have been the most insane floor planning experiment I had ever seen.

I was conducting a five day class on using and managing web application servers. The students were twelve web developers. My classroom was their 'work bay.' They worked in a large room, and each person had their desk along a perimeter of the room, facing the wall. There were no dividers between the employees, save for two large filing cabinets which jutted out and obscured a couple of the developers from my vantage point.

I was in the middle of the room, lecturing with a projected presentation on one wall. All the developers turned their chairs around and faced me like a room of eager kindergarteners.

During one break I heard an awful sound—like a dentist drilling on a helpless victim! The noise was annoying to say the least. I looked around and no one seemed to take much notice (though a few screwed up their faces in disapproval at the noise). I went behind one of the large filing cabinets where a lone developer was hunched up in his corner. Lo and behold, he had an old (and loud!) Latte machine and was grinding coffee and doing other sorts of obnoxious chemistry experiments to produce various coffee concoctions!

I only had to lecture in that room for a week, but the developers I left behind work there year round. How they ever got anything done or kept their sanity is beyond me!

■ CONFIGURATION MANAGEMENT

Why use a version control tool? Doesn't it introduce administrative overhear? Yes it does—but it is well worth it!

There are several benefits. It reduces human error. It makes sure code is in a common location. The status of the code should be well understood—is it finished, is it being modified, has it been tested and ready to check in? Even for an individual developer working on a lot of files, it's easy to lose track of what files you've changed. Version control tools reduce human error and increase productivity.

Many version control tools can be configured to prompt for comments with code check in. In this manner, software becomes self-documenting by virtue of the configuration management in place.

When pulling in code from several team members, the last thing you want is is to have incorrect versions of code being included and causing problems. Proper use of version control and configuration management tools eliminate the heartache of running down problems just because someone erroneously copied in a test file.

At a practical level version control tools provide not only a documentation mechanism, but also prevent multiple people from accidentally modifying the same piece of code.

Another practical feature in version control tools is the ability to compare revisions. Look at the file history. If something works one day, but the next day it breaks, quickly find the troublesome code by using the configuration management tool to view the difference between the two versions of the file.

> **With version control, you can identify changes and solve problems quickly.**

Even though there are some fairly sophisticated tools out there, the most basic tools will provide the core lock and unlock and basic versioning features that are needed. There are some inexpensive—often free!—tools to use. There's no excuse to not to use version tools.

Version control has to be to planned for. If version control tools aren't in place, include implementing a version control tool to the project plan.

Make sure to have a backup scheme appropriate for the development environment. It is one thing to have the file server with the version control repository backed up. But if developers are checking out software to their local workstations and have a hard drive failure you could lose several days worth of productivity.

■ THREE ENVIRONMENTS

Create three separate environments for developing software: one for developers only, one for external personnel to beta test code during the quality assurance phase, and finally a production environment to deploy the software to end users.

Having only two environments—a developer environment and a production environment—is an Achilles' Heel. If everyone wrote perfect code and there were never any changes, two environments would suffice. But developers implement code, test code, and then, after viewing the results, make additional changes. Meanwhile, the people doing quality assurance are still testing.

Separate environments are necessary to make sure developers have the freedom to make changes and do unit testing, while quality assurance testing occurs in a static environment. Nothing is more frustrating than trying to do quality assurance when the code is changing right before your eyes!

■ DEFECT TRACKING

Another major component of software development is tracking the various errors detected in the software. This is known as defect tracking.

There are many software tools that do this—both commercial and open source, freeware software tools that are very effective.

Many issues about software flaws are reported either by a developer or end users, emailing in a description of the problem. Manually trying to copy the problem description from the email to another piece of software is time consuming. Instead, use an email based workflow.

In a ticket tracking system with an email gateway, it's easy to take an email describing an issue you have received from an end user and forward the email to an address such as 'bugs@mycompany.com.' A ticket tracking system with an email gateway can immediately log this issue into a database for tracking.

> ### *Tales from the Trenches*
>
> *'Let's call it Project Enabled Team Environment— PETE for short!' I emailed out to my team. The name stuck, and soon hundreds of our clients were notified in a marketing blitz about our new way to manage projects.*
>
> *We had just spent a few weeks putting together a consolidated issue tracking and project management system. It was all web based, using email to receive and notify team members about issues, bugs, new features—in short, any and all workflow tasks for software development.*
>
> *Our customers loved it. It was tremendously powerful to send an email to the IT department, be assigned a tracking number instantly, and know that the IT team was alerted to the issue.*
>
> *PETE came to mean to our clients "No more issues will fall through the cracks." Users logged in to view reports about our systems status, the current reported defects, and which team members were working on which tasks.*
>
> *Over time, PETE became almost human. We talked about it as if it were another member of our project team: "I don't know—why don't you check with PETE?"*
>
> *PETE helped us manage customer expectations. Our open-book approach was gratifying—people trusted us because we didn't hide anything. PETE responded and logged all problems, even on weekends and the middle of the night.*

Some people even choose to combine defect tracking with project management requirements into one seamless process—defect tracking that flows into a task management system. This way there is one repository that tracks individual tasks, defects, and change requests, giving you one database in which to manage the task queue. This yields a tremendous time savings!

■ SOP DOCUMENTATION

Standard operating procedure (SOP) documentation should be built incrementally during the software development life cycle. All the major components of the system should be well documented before your system goes into production, especially if you're using a new core piece of software like an application server, a different database or a new web server.

How should the web server be configured? How is it restarted? How should the application server be tuned? How do your database and backups run? All these basic things need to be well understood, and well documented. Doing this incrementally throughout the development phase of the project will help you have a seamless transition to production.

■ EMPOWER DEVELOPERS

When team members are scattered throughout different departments, it can become time-consuming to get even minor changes implemented.

Developers should be empowered with a certain amount of systems administration control within the development environment. This way servers can be configured and restarted at will. Developers need to be able to quickly act so they do not get log jammed and become unproductive while waiting for a systems administrator to make some minor change for them.

Of course, the quality assurance environment, by necessity must be locked down. Your systems configuration and standard operating procedures will need to be well documented. When you move from development to QA, you will quickly find out if the developer hasn't documented system changes needed to run the application properly. Have this separation of system privileges flush out undocumented systems settings.

■ DAILY SMOKE TEST

On bigger projects, use something known as a 'smoke test.' Just like the early days when people soldered together circuit boards then tested them to see if they smoked, IT likewise needs to wire together systems and check for smoke early on!

> ***The best status report is working software.***

Today, especially in the larger software development projects, implementing a daily or weekly smoke test is invaluable. Have team members who are working on individual modules or software components periodically check in their code at a specified time. This is code they have tested that they believe works. After developers check their work in you do a build of the software. Compile all the pieces together and designate someone on the team to do a walkthrough to make sure all the components fit together and things seem to work properly.

If things break, unexpected changes made by developers will be readily apparent. Smoke tests allow these issues to be detected early on so you don't end up at the end of the project having major incompatibilities between sub-systems in the software.

Chapter 12 Summary

Build the Best Environment

- Give developers the environment they need.
- Make sure your developers get long periods of time to concentrate on their work.

Configuration Management

- Make sure the code is in a common location.
- Flag the status of the code.
- Leverage the ability to compare revisions.
- Prevent multiple people from accidentally modifying the same piece of code.

Three Environments

- Create three separate environments:
  1) Development environment
  2) Test/QA environment
  3) Production environment

Defect Tracking

- Track errors detected in the software.

SOP Documentation

- Develop standard operating procedures (SOPs).

Empower Developers

- Enable developers to have systems administration control within the development environment.

Daily Smoke Test

- Periodically do a software build ensuring all components compile and work properly.

13

Divide and Conquer

I n the development phase of the project, dividing the team members into groups with similar strengths will boost productivity.

■ UI VS. BUSINESS LOGIC

Depending on the project size, you may want to divide the development team into two groups—a user interface group focusing more on the creative design of the user interface, and the business logic developers, who work on more of the business rules, database access, and systems integration tasks.

There are some people who have very good creative design instinct. You may even need to draw this talent from a design person outside of the IT department. Many of the smartest programmers I know have little skill in creating an aesthetically appealing web design! Proactively segmenting your team into user interface design versus the business logic developers will help in developing systems which work well and look good at the same time.

Tales from the Trenches

"I never did like to design web pages," the developer told me, grinning with delight.

Our project was big enough that this developer had been assigned to a business logic group—they dealt strictly with business rules, talking to the database, and creating an API the user interface team could call.

I wandered over to the design team that was eagerly crafting the new look and feel to our web system. "We're using the corporate colors and logo, but adapting it to work within our new, web design guidelines. Management is going to be blown away with how slick this looks!" I peered over the graphics design person and agreed. It was one slick looking web application!

Fortunately, our team was large, and we had the highest caliber talent. The design team with a smattering of programming talent, and our business logic group, with their hard core backend systems skills, were each having the time of their life exercising their skills to implement a gorgeous system that met our business requirements.

Looks aren't everything. But packaging is important, as any product manager will tell you. The success of our project was later judged not just on it's ability to work correctly, but also because it looked good, and people were proud to show off our system!

■ DOCUMENTATION

Who will do the documentation for your software? In some software development models—client/server software, packaged software, and large, complicated ERP systems—there's a strong emphasis on thorough documentation.

The need for documentation has drastically decreased with the advent of web applications. This is largely because the web has enforced a simplified set of user interface capabilities to the end-user.

Just think about how many times you have gone to a web site and placed an order for a product. Before you did that, did you have to go read a set of elaborate instructions before you could place the order? Did you have to consult the online help to use the system? Online help is seldom needed. Successful web sites are intuitive—users can use them without help—even though the user interface look and feel is extremely different from one web site to another.

The web presents a limited set of widgets that you can use on your page. There are dropdown lists and edit boxes and just a few widgets that are easy to understand, that users are familiar with. There are no hidden features like drag and drop and right mouse click that are unintuitive and confuse end users.

Web systems may not be as fast to use as their client/server software counterparts, but they are straightforward and easy to understand. In most traditional, PC based software I've implemented, creating thorough user documentation was a must. Users often had to be trained extensively before they could even begin to be productive. When is the last time you had to go through training before filling out a web form or ordering a product online?

While you may still need a minimal set of documentation for your system, don't expect it to consume much of your project's resources.

■ INTEGRATING COMPONENTS AND WEB SERVICES

If your software development project is large and complex, particularly if there are requirements to integrate with other systems, it is helpful to break these integration tasks out as separate projects.

Let's say for example you have a mainframe system with which you need to integrate to complete one portion of your project. Break this integration effort out as a separate project. Run it parallel to your main development effort. In this way you treat those other integration efforts somewhat as black boxes. Define an API, were you have the data and function calls established and documented.

If necessary, you can create a dummy piece of software, a 'stub' piece of software, that you call from within your code. Your main development team can charge ahead and not wait on this separate integration project to finish up. Once the integration team has completed their side of the project, the main team will integrate and test their interfaces to these backend systems.

Decoupling integration projects eases the complexity of managing various software development efforts.

Chapter 13 Summary

UI vs. Business Logic

- Consider dividing the development team into two groups—a user interface group and business logic developers.

Documentation

- Decide what kind of documentation your system will need.

- Most web systems require only minimal documentation due to the limited, standardized widget sets of web pages.

Integrating Components and web Services

- If there are requirements to integrate with other systems, break these integration tasks out as separate projects.

14

Managing Development

Think of someone you've known who has successfully managed a web project. What gave them the ability to succeed? Chance and good circumstances give you the occasional successful project. But to repeatedly, systematically ensure your projects come in on time, under budget, and meet business objectives, there are some concrete techniques you can use to manage the development phase successfully.

■ MANAGE TO RESULTS

Know the difference between managing and administering. The mediocre team leader knows how to administer. The successful team leader knows how to *manage*.

Make sure your project doesn't get bogged down in the 'busy work tasks' of project administration. Project details quickly bog you down. Wallowing in the quagmire of complex project plans and fancy reports does not help if your project is fundamentally off base.

Think about outcomes. What is the goal is of the project? Are you meeting the goal? Is there a better, quicker way to accomplish the same thing?

Sometimes during the midst of the project, it is advantageous to make major, fundamental adjustments to your project plan. If you manage to results, your eye is on the goal and making whatever course corrections are necessary to get you there.

Don't feel constrained by your project plan. Most project plans are somewhat arbitrary to begin with. In the midst of your project if you see a shortcut, take it. Focus on the goal. Throw your project plan out the window if you need to.

I've stopped some projects mid-stream. A commercial package was just released that met the business objectives of the software we were developing in-house that made our project obsolete. Was this the right thing to do? Absolutely. It met the project goal (our objective statement) and made good sense to the company. Some team leaders are too infatuated with implementing their technology to be alert for such opportunities. Do not let this happen to you!

A great measure of true management is the granularity of your reporting. The novice manager does not appreciate the difference between information and knowledge. Stakeholders and upper management only care about summarized knowledge—is the project on course, on time and on budget? Are we meeting our objectives? They are not concerned about minutia like coding issues, lines of code produced and technical hurdles you have run across.

I target my project status reports <u>to be no</u> more than a page in length. Often three sentences will do. Avoid the excess busy work of detailed project plans crafted largely to impress superiors.

Be bold, be innovative. Meet your business objectives even if it means having to chunk your project plan or even scuttle the project mid-stream. Communicate your progress succinctly, in business terms, to stakeholders. Your project will succeed, and the recognition you achieve will advance your career!

■ USE SURGICAL OVERTIME

I had a senior developer once tell me, "no matter how hard you plan, it always seems like the last two weeks of a project you work like crazy to try to get the project finished on time!" That's often true because of the *way* the typical project is managed.

If your project is starting to slip, use what Fergus O'Connell coined as "surgical overtime" to get the project back on track. Surgical overtime is simply requiring developers early in the project—*before* things get out of hand—to work normal hours plus a small amount of overtime to get the project back on track. By spreading the pain early in the project, and if need be over multiple instances across several multiple weeks in small, bite-sized chunks, it's much easier to get the work done. It is easier to get the extra time out of people and the morale is much higher than the often used alternative—waiting for the end of the project and trying to put in 70 and 80 hours a week in a mad blitz of desperation.

So how do you get people to work surgical overtime? Tap into developer motivations. Talk to your team in terms of achievement and recognition. Demonstrate how it's going to benefit the company—and their career—to get the project done on time and done right. As the team succeeds, each individual is going to receive recognition. At review time such achievements will not be forgotten.

When you ask a developer for surgical overtime, ask for something reasonable. Ask for small, do-able chunks of time. Sometimes it's not even extra time, it's simply extra effort. A short lunch and an intense couple of days (without interruptions!) is sometimes all it takes to get back on track.

It is part of good management to walk around and know what your teammates are doing. Make an effort to work around people's schedules. Because you're asking for over-time *earlier* in the project, you're not as pressed to have it done immediately. When it turns out they have a packed schedule and their family time is such that it is difficult to give you time that week, be flexible. Let someone else do the work, or save the work until later.

When you're asking for surgical overtime, make sure you then reward people with a break later. Quality team members work hard—but they're going to still need an occasional break. Make sure you balance work and personal life—for yourself as well as the people on the team. I've seen people be workaholics, working 60 to 70 hour weeks with regularity. Don't let people work excessively and to the point of burnout. Ultimately, that's bad for them and bad for your team. Make sure people work reasonable hours.

Give comp time as appropriate. If people know that extra time worked now will result in some time off when the project is over, people won't feel cheated.

Use other rewards to incent your team members. If you're asking your people to work after hours, stay there with them. Order pizza, give them comp time, buy them free movie tickets—use any and all perks in your power to make your team feel valued. Moral will soar, and your team will march toward success!

■ BREAK LOG JAMS

Build roaming time into your schedule. Make sure that you walk around, speak with your team, instant message people working remotely—constantly have your finger on the pulse of what's going on with your team. When things come up—when people express frustrations over a problem or they mention a bottleneck they've run into—you're immediately aware of it and can quickly marshal whatever resources are needed to solve the problem.

Most of these are not major roadblocks to the project requiring massive attention. Sometimes it is simply a basic issue—"I'm having a problem with a piece of code and I've been working on it four hours. I don't know what's wrong." Make sure you take a personal look at the problem. Recruit someone else on the team to come brainstorm a solution.

Tales from the Trenches

A Boston company called my consulting firm in Dallas, seeking a technical expert to come in and help them with a technical bottleneck they just couldn't overcome. They wanted an outsider—someone who could solve their problem—as their project deadlines continued to slip and become an embarrassment.

I arrived, driving through the snowy New England countryside to their corporate campus. After brief introductions I spent a few hours with some of their developers reviewing the root of their problem. Their web

> *application server had an odd compiler issue that produced errors when running their (supposedly) perfectly good, syntactically correct Java code.*
>
> *Six hours later I had identified the pesky issue—there was a bug in the compiler itself incorrectly interpreting certain code comments as machine instructions. This caused unpredictable (and disruptive) run time behaviors.*
>
> *We simply eliminated the troublesome comment tags and enforced a new standard comments style. Within three days, the issue which had caused multiple projects and nearly twenty developers to bang their head against the walls for three months was solved!*
>
> *Moral of the story? Create a slush fund to tackle bottlenecks which can and do arise. Plan on problems and spare yourself the pain of delayed projects and overrun budgets. Spending a few thousand dollars for a code-wise commando to come in and break up technical logjams is money well spent!*

Demonstrate your problem-solving capability. Once you've shown the reason you're asking about them is genuine concern, your team will realize it is not your hidden agenda to micromanage them, but rather to know what's going on so you can help.

Become known as a problem solver your team can call on. Let people know your willingness to marshal your talents and the combined resources of your team to quickly and efficiently solve problems.

Two heads are definitely better than one, and sometimes one plus one equal three. Just having another set of eyes looking at an issue will often quickly remedy the problem.

Be the 'Go To' Person

Your responsibility as a project manager is to be a problem solver and to know about logjams. Deal with complaints. Hear frustrations of team members. If things are going on in your team that need to be addressed, make sure you know about them and do your best to solve those problems.

Learn the culture, perceptions and attitudes of your team. Some people are just dour—it's not that there's really a problem, they're just one to complain about everything. Understanding the culture of your team is going to help you know and manage your people.

Maximize the amount of communication going on within your team. Many times communication is challenging, especially with distributed work teams. The periodic phone calls, the five-minute walk around the office, e-mailing the group with a team update multiple times a week, instant messaging people, hanging around the water cooler—all these things help facilitate communication within the group and give you visibility to what's really going on with your team.

Be A Roaming Project Manager

Make sure you stay in contact with the senior stakeholders—the people who funded this project. Understand what their responsibilities are, and what their perception of the project is. Be present on client calls and sales calls. Be in sales meetings, and try to understand why this project is being funded, and who the end users are who are going to use the system. Do whatever you need to do to understand the business reasons driving the project. This knowledge will help you align your project's objectives with your company's business objectives.

Don't be the project manager who takes the project specifications and isn't seen again until the project completion! If you do this, when you roll out the software, you may find out there are new unexpected issues that jeopardize the success of the project.

Pitfalls awaiting the project manager who is not astute include: expectations that weren't set correctly, a misunderstanding about what the project requirements really were, or executive infighting which makes your project's outcome 'politically incorrect.' If you as project manager have good visibility to the overall high level business needs and business environment, a lot of these things can be avoided.

Differentiate yourself by truly *understanding* your company's business, and navigate to project success!

Chapter 14 Summary

Manage to Results

- Differentiate between managing and administering.

Use Surgical Overtime

- Before things get out of hand, work a minimal amount of overtime to get the project back on track.

Break Log Jams

- Stay close to your team; marshal your talents and the combined resources of your team to quickly and efficiently solve problems.

Step 4

Deploy

Success is the sum of small efforts – repeated
day in and day out.

— Robert Collier

15
Beat Business Rivals by Testing

In the previous section, we talked about the development phase of the software development life cycle. As the project moves into the deployment phase, it's time to begin planning for the move into production.

Managing your project in web time requires a good job of orchestrating this effort—doing adequate unit testing and planning ahead so quality assurance testers are ready with a well crafted test plan in hand, ready to evaluate the system as soon as the developers wrap up the code.

■ UNIT TESTING

The initial, and most effective means of testing begins during the middle of the project. Developers do their own individual testing of their code before they deploy it to the group. This individual unit testing (testing your own unit or module first before deploying it to the group) is essential, but is often overlooked by developers overeager to whip out code.

More than once I've seen lousy code slammed out into the code repository without even a rudimentary test by the developer! How do you prevent this?

One way is have intermittent code swaps. As mentioned earlier, code reviews and code swaps begin early in the project life cycle. Testing and quality assurance is an integral, ongoing part of the entire development process.

When developers finish a section of their assignment that is at a logical breaking point—reassign it to another team member! Having a new developer inherit the code in the middle of the project may be daunting, but it encourages collaboration and cross-training.

> ***Use 'code swaps' to expose code to other team members.***

Eliminate sloppy code by quickly exposing it to other team members. Code swaps are an alternate mechanism to pair programming (where two developers sit in front of a single computer and write code) and group code reviews (where code is ponderously stepped through line-by-line.) While code swaps and code reviews actually begin early in the project, they become particularly important at project's end as a final step in the quality assurance process.

After a couple of times of being ridiculed by team members about sloppy code, developers soon bring their standards of code writing to a higher level, or find themselves looking for a less-demanding vocation!

■ QUALITY ASSURANCE (QA)

The code is written and reviewed, but does it really do what it's supposed to do? You need to find out before the end users do! Ideally, if your staff is large enough, you will have a quality assurance group, a team dedicated to doing quality assurance testing on software. Even if it's not a dedicated group, it's advisable to have someone besides the developers who wrote the code do the testing. Wisdom says, "Don't let the fox guard the hen house!"

One of the nice things about web architecture is that it's extremely easy to provide access to quality assurance testers. As long as testers have a web browser they can quickly access your software. As they find bugs, you can go through short, rapid cycles of collecting a set of bug reports, fixing the bugs, and getting it back to the quality assurance users for another iteration of testing.

A quality assurance test plan is needed to begin testing. One convenient system is to use the use cases you created earlier in the project to form the basis of your quality assurance test plan. Number the use cases and actions in each use case. As the tester finds issues, they log the issue and reference the specific use case action.

As you prepare to test, make sure to have the test database set up and configured to support all the various scenarios that will be tested. Try to do some basic capacity planning by creating a large volume of data in the database. A lot of times, developers just have a small amount of data in their test database. The application seems to perform well. By adding even a marginal amount of data you quickly expose performance issues. Many times code doesn't execute as planned because it doesn't scale well with production database volumes.

■ PUTTING SITE PERFORMANCE TO THE TEST

Previously we talked about doing thin-slice testing—taking each of the architectural components in your system and wiring them together, making sure from an end-to-end perspective your system will actually work as planned. Knowing that the system components work is not enough though—you need to validate that the system will work as expected *under load*. As you perform quality assurance testing, if your web site is going to have a large amount of traffic, create a capacity test plan that will simulate load on your software architecture.

Tales from the Trenches

'Why does the page take so long to load? It worked so great in our demos!'

The manager from the Wall Street brokerage was visibly frustrated. They had just spent a lot of money to implement the internal financial application. Now that it was in production in use by hundreds of personnel, it was quickly turning into an embarrassment. I had flown in as a consultant to review the system and answer this troublesome question.

I reported to them:"When you did your testing, you only had a few hundred rows of data in your database. Now that the system is in production, your actual data has swelled to hundreds of thousand of rows. The transactions join across these large tables. Unfortunately, you can only solve this by re-architecting the database and re-writing the code."

> *My answer was honest, but not particularly well received. In the end they took the project totally off line for another two months while they made major changes.*
>
> *Moral of the story? Make sure you test with real-world conditions; don't wait until your users start taxing the system!*

Before creating a capacity test plan, you'll want to compile assumptions about how many end users will be hitting the web site, and what peak traffic and spikes would look like. If you're doing e-commerce, for example, it may be that during the holiday season there is ten times as much traffic as during a normal week. You'll need to have assumptions put together about what production usage will look like, and then implement software tools to simulate this level of load.

Done properly, this can be time consuming! If scalability is a mission critical requirement, make sure to include the time and expense to do stress testing into your project plan.

■ LAST MINUTE PREPARATIONS

The Release Manager

When determining who the release manager will be, bear in mind that it may not be the project manager. The release manager is someone familiar with the system's design, the database schema changes that have to happen, and the software installation procedure. The release manager should be someone who has an attention to detail. This person is responsible for compiling the release notes—outlining the new features and changes occurring within the release.

Version Labels

The release manager may also be in charge of the version control tool. Use standardized versioning labels on the software. One common convention is to use the first digit to designate a major release. A 1.00 release is the first release. Future minor enhancements to the 1.00 release increment the first decimal, so 1.10 and 1.20 versions indicate by their label a release with new features.

The third decimal indicates no new features but a bug fix. So if your 1.1 release goes out, and there's a bug you quickly identify and fix, the new fixed version is flagged as the 1.11 release. In this way the software label gives an indication of what the release contains.

Having well labeled releases, with release notes detailing the release contents and technical considerations, allows your team to manage current and prior versions with efficiency. If a bug appears, the version control system can be searched for older versions of the software where the issue may have been introduced.

Signoff Process

Implement a release signoff form. This mechanism ensures all parties affected by the release have sufficient notification. You don't want to release a piece of software only to find some other department scrambling because they didn't know about the change and it's affected them in some way.

A release form is a mechanism to ensure that impacted people are notified in advance and that the stakeholders have approved the software to be released to end users.

Include the name of the project, the version number, and the impact of the change on the release signoff form.

Getting proper approvals on the signoff form helps you think about what other systems will be impacted. Include on the form all resources needed to release the software.

> ***Following a simple process like a release signoff form ensures everyone is on the same page for the software release.***

In some situations this might seem to be overly bureaucratic—if this process is overkill, then simply send out an email to the affected departments well in advance.

Release Checklist

A generic release checklist is used for each software release. It is a list of all the things that need to happen: updating version control, labeling the software release, verifying any debugging flags or any test codes in place for testing are removed, and removing unused files.

Install/Uninstall Plans

The release checklist will make sure you've put together an installation plan that spells out in detail what software needs to go where, which files are located in which directories, and which database changes need to happen. This installation plan also forms the basis of a roll-back plan. If things go wrong and unexpected bugs occur, how do you roll back the release to the prior version? Make sure you have an uninstall plan mapped out in advance.

Before installing a release affecting an existing production environment, always do a trial run installing the software release in a test environment. Install all the components according to the installation plan, and then do an uninstall to make sure you can roll back the changes to their previous state. By implementing these safeguards, you can go into the actual production release with confidence about having a successful deployment.

Chapter 15 Summary

Unit Testing

- Have intermittent 'code swaps' to prevent poor coding.

Quality Assurance (QA)

- Develop a quality assurance test plan.

- Have the test database set up and configured to support all the various scenarios needed to test.

Putting Site Performance to the Test

- Expand 'thin-slice' testing by stress testing the site.

- Develop assumptions about how many end users will be hitting the web site, when there will be peak traffic and what seasonal spikes there may be.

Doing the Release

- Designate an individual to be the release manager.

- Define a standardized version labeling convention, and put every release under version control.

- Create a release signoff form and signoff process to ensure all affected parties have sufficient notification.

16

Trouble Free Systems

Once the software is packaged and tested, release it with confidence. Prepare an infrastructure to deal with supporting and managing day-to-day operations.

■ PLANNING FOR DOWN TIME

What level of downtime is acceptable for the system? For some companies, being down for even a few minutes is extremely expensive including the loss of orders or, even worse, the loss of consumer confidence as users see your web site unavailable. For other companies, being down for an hour does not incur loss of revenue or loss of reputation.

The Cost of Availability

Evaluate the true business cost of having an outage. It's easy for an executive to say "we want zero downtime," but is the cost to have a highly available system really justified?

There are many technologies available to reduce downtime: having multiple redundant servers, using load balancers, and having redundant network providers. You can even implement geographic failure where there are multiple data centers with mirrored web sites. In the case that one data center is down through a network failure or hardware crash, the system rolls over to an Internet data center located in another region of the country.

These things are technically possible, but consider if the cost justifies such an expensive solution.

Tales from the Trenches

I was doing an audit for the financial services firm. They had just made an expensive mistake, and they were scrambling to recover.

'We were off line with one of our biggest customers for almost three days!' The manager was trying to piece together his reputation; having my team independently audit his systems was part of his plan for redemption.

I listened and asked questions to learn how this happened. The company hosted the e-commerce site for a major retailer, and transactions went completely off-line for three days. They had redundant servers, re-dundant networks—a textbook high-end e-commerce system.

In the end it was a simple mistake that did them in. Their DNS records were only set to update every three days, and a low-level tech had accidentally made a typo in their web address settings. By the time they determined what was wrong, their DNS settings had propagated throughout the Internet, and it took up to several days in some cases for the problem to be com-pletely repaired.

Moral of the story? There is no such thing as a zero down time web site. Even the biggest sites have their problems from time to time!

Maintenance Windows

Production software inevitably needs maintenance. One way to determine when and how it can be done is through analysis of prior user traffic.

Define a scheduled maintenance policy so that everyone knows when changes to a production system can be deployed.

I often send out an email to my customers a week in advance of any systems changes. The day of the change I post a message to the web site alerting users to the planned outage later in the day.

During the maintenance, users see this message:

> **Service Temporarily Unavailable**
>
> 'This web site is down for routine mainte-
> nance. We apologize for any inconvenience.
> Please try again later.'

Give users adequate advance notice of scheduled down-time. Doing this sets expectations and avoids embarrassing issues of surprise software installations.

■ MANAGING DAY TO DAY OPERATIONS

Once the system is successfully deployed there are some tricks you can use to monitor and manage it with a mini-mum of hassle—and make yourself look good in the process!

Have software monitoring all systems you deploy. You never want a superior or a customer to be the first one to know a system is down!

There are many software monitoring packages that check the status of a web server, application server, database and other system components. You may need to write custom software to get visibility to the various components of your system, but gaining full visibility to the status of your system is absolutely critical.

Automatically monitor systems, and tie in a realtime no-tification system so that whoever's on call is notified if there are issues. I like to have system alerts sent to my email, so during business hours I see immediately when there are problems.

■ WHEN SOMETHING
GOES WRONG

A defined and published support policy must be in place before releasing the software. What is the on-call schedule for those supporting the release? Is there a two tiered support structure, with less skilled front-line support personnel, and developers called in only at a last resort? If so, under what circumstances does the help desk contact your support team? If you want to be able to call on one of your programmers at 1am on a Sunday, you'll want to alert them to this possibility in advance!

Building a well thought out support infrastructure eliminates the hassle that the responsibility of supporting production software often brings.

A support web site serves as the first line resource for end users needing assistance. Automated FAQ builders, an automated trouble ticket system, technical documents on issues they encounter—these can be built over time and reduce the time and frustration incurred in supporting web systems.

If something goes wrong, whom should end users contact? The developer on call needs to have vendor contact information available.

Consider what sort of escalation procedure is needed. If there is monitoring software looking at the status of the systems, it can be configured to e-mail or page the on call person when problems arise. One trick is to have software configured so that if no one responds to a page after a predetermined period of time, it escalates to the next person in a hunt group. It will continue to try different people, wait, and then seek the next person on the list until someone responds. The person working the issue checks off a form in the software to alert the system (and others that may be checking into the issue) that they've responded and are working the issue.

I knew of one company whose escalation logic was set up to first page the people on call. If it couldn't find them, it would page the developers. If still no one had responded it would eventually escalate all the way up to the CEO! That's quite an incentive for developers to make sure they follow their on-call schedule!

■ DEALING WITH CHANGE

Once software is deployed, you will be receiving feedback from the end users. Collect these responses into a ticket tracking system. While some requests may be related to system bugs, many will be feature requests. People will want to start seeing an enhancement to the software. So how do you deal with change?

Deal with end users in a similar contractual fashion. While their job may be to get the best and most feature rich software to do their job, your responsibility is to filter those requests, get them prioritized by stakeholders, and roll them out in a controlled, budgeted and scheduled fashion.

When end users ask for these changes, there needs to be a defined channel for change requests to funnel through—some party that makes decisions on those change requests, prioritizes them, decides which ones are worthy of implementing, and approves a budget to implement those changes.

Change Request Form

I like to require end users to fill out a change request form. I've noticed that by simply putting up this minor bureaucratic hurdle, I cut down on 50% or more of the change requests.

> ***People that don't care enough about a feature to fill out a change request form are obviously not passionate about getting that feature!***

A change request form should include the software name, the date, who is requesting the change, and what the business value or return on investment will be if the change is implemented.

While this information may only be used internally, it can be valuable to take stock of *who* requested a change, and what the positive impact will be. At some point you call stakeholders together and review these various change requests. If the same feature has been asked for multiple times by multiple people, then chances are that feature is something you'll want to consider implementing!

Change Control Board

Consider creating a change control board (CCB). A change control board is a group typically spanning different functional areas within your company. It includes the stakeholders who determine if a feature request is really valid, if it's really important to the company, and whether it's worth funding.

Having a change control board is a powerful way of arbitrating the flood of request from end users that come in.

Without such controls, I've often seen IT groups run amok, developing any features that came in and seemed good, not always cognizant of true positive impact to the company's bottom line.

Studies have shown that the typical software project grows by about 40 percent during the course of a project. Why is this? It is usually because end users (and stakeholders!) constantly come in and continue to dump feature requests upon the development team. When the project finally does roll out, it is late and woefully over budget. Have a change control board and carefully manage the flow and approval of change requests. Keep projects on course—and save your reputation as being a project manager who can deliver.

> ***The typical software project grows by about 40 percent during the course of a project. Avoid this scope creep!***

The reason end users tend to make these change requests so passionately is because they're used to longer projects and one-shot projects—they think if they don't get their feature implemented now, it may never see the light of day. When you are systematic about rolling out releases every three months or less, you change the expectations of the end user community. Let them know their feature will be considered for a future release, possibly as early as the next three month release cycle, all depending on the authorization you receive from your change control board!

Chapter 16 Summary

Planning for Down Time

- Define the true cost of having your systems unavailable.

- Define the amount of acceptable downtime, given your business model and budget.

- Identify acceptable maintenance release windows.

- Give users adequate advance notice of scheduled downtime.

Managing Day-to-Day Operations

- Implement software to monitor systems.

- Configure realtime notification system so on-call staff are notified instantly of production issues.

When Something Goes Wrong

- Publish a support policy with escalation procedures.

- Create a well thought out support infrastructure.

Dealing with Change

- Change will happen—plan for it.

- Create a change request form and change control board (CCB) to manage change requests.

Afterword

After every long voyage of adventure, it's always refreshing to put your ship into port, and take a breather.

Now your software is deployed. Your development team has worked hard to successfully deliver this software. It's time to lighten up the work load and assess the project you have just completed. Congratulate your team. Take them out to lunch and celebrate!

Use this opportunity to learn from your mistakes. Have a meeting to compile a set of lessons you have learned. What new technologies did you implement? What things do you need to do differently next time? What mistakes did you make? Which team members went beyond the call of duty to exceed expectations? Who grew the most and learned new skills or took on new responsibilities?

Refine your project methodology, and in doing so give your entire team a sense of growth. Seek to build upon your recent experience to learn and innovate. By doing this, you foster a process of continuous improvement which leads you to achieve new and future goals.

Business is thirty percent patience.

— Chinese proverb

Index

Order Form

🖶	**Web Orders:**	http://www.stanshinn.com
🖨	**Fax Orders:**	888-432-5796. Send this form.
📄	**Email Orders:**	orders@stanshinn.com
✉	**Postal Orders:**	RareClarity
		120 East FM 544
		Suite 72 PMB 354
		Murphy, TX 75094

Please send the following books, disks or reports. I understand that I may return any of them for a full refund within 30 days.

____

____

Please send more FREE information on:

Speaking/Seminars   Mailing List   Consulting

Name: ____

Address:____

City: ________________________ State: ________ ZIP: ____________-________

Telephone: __________________ Email Address: ________________________

Sales Tax: please add 8.25% for products shipped to Texas addresses.

Shipping & Handling: US: $4 for the first book or disk and $2 for each additional product. International: $9 for first book or disk; $5 for each additional product (estimate).

Payment: Check   Credit Card   (circle one)
Visa   MasterCard   AMEX   Discover

Card number:____

Name on card: ________________________________ Exp. Date: ______ / ______

www.ingramcontent.com/pod-product-compliance
Lightning Source LLC
Chambersburg PA
CBHW022202050726
47590CB00002B/617